# THE MOST VISIBLE CHURCH

'When some divines were disputing before Charles II, about the visible Church, he turned their attention to that of Harrow On The Hill which has ever since been called The Visible Church'.

*Daniel Lysons, The Environs of London*

'**H** *allowed pile our fathers raised*
**A** *ncient fane where God is praised*
**R** *esting place of saints of old*
**R** *efuge of the living God*
**O** *h may ages yet to come*
**W** *orship in this sacred home*

'**C** *rown of all the neighbouring lands*
**H** *igh and lifted up it stands*
**U** *nto Heaven its lofty finger*
**R** *aised, forbids us here to linger*
**C** *alling with its silent voice*
**H** *eaven or hell awaits thy choice*'

*S. Scott*

# THE MOST VISIBLE CHURCH

## The first 900 years of St Mary's, Harrow On The Hill

BY

DON WALTER

THIS BOOK HAS BEEN MADE POSSIBLE
BY A GENEROUS DONATION FROM KODAK LTD

BARON
MCMXCIV

PUBLISHED BY BARON BIRCH FOR QUOTES LIMITED
AND PRODUCED BY KEY COMPOSITION, SOUTH MIDLANDS LITHOPLATES,
HILLMAN PRINTERS (FROME) LIMITED, CHENEY & SONS AND
WBC BOOKBINDERS LIMITED

ISBN 0 86023 554 8

# CONTENTS

# ACKNOWLEDGEMENTS

The following are just a few of the people who have helped to make the writing of this book both possible — and pleasurable: the Rev Ron Swan, Vicar of St Mary's and his Vicar's Warden, John Lampitt, for their constant encouragement; Bob Thomson, Harrow Local History Archivist, not only for loaning valuable material but also for reading the text; Alisdair Hawkyard, Harrow School Archivist and the Governors of Harrow School for their courtesy in allowing the author access to the treasures of the Archive Room and Vaughan Library, and especially to Tracy Bohane, for so cheerfully — and accurately — typing the text.

*The author would also like to acknowledge the skill with which virtually all the illustrations have been copied from often inadequate originals by the photographic department of the Harrow Observer; also the talents of their gifted young photographer, Sophie Powell, who has taken most of the contemporary pictures.*

# INTRODUCTION

If it is hard to believe that St Mary's, Harrow On The Hill — our St Mary's — is now 900 years old; it may be even harder to credit that this is, in fact, the very first book to attempt to tell the complete history of those years.

It is thus a task that has been approached with considerable awe by its essentially layman-author; indeed, its planning, research and writing has taken almost as many years as it took Lanfranc to build the first church on the Hill.

There have, of course, been earlier writings about St Mary's. The 800th anniversary, for example, was the occasion for both Samuel Gardner's *Architectural History* and Done Bushell's *Octo-Centenary Tracts*. But invaluable as their genuine scholarship has been in the creation of this volume, the first gives us, in reality, only an extended architectural tour; the latter consists of events and personalities described in isolation rather than in sequence and then, only as far as the Reformation.

What has always seemed to be lacking — and what is modestly attempted here — is a narrative that places all that is known of local events not only in proper chronological order but also in some kind of historical context to convey some small idea of what was happening in the larger world outside.

Inevitably, the need to encompass such a narrative within the confines of one relatively slender volume has meant huge gaps, considerable assumptions and, not infrequently, a child's history-primer approach to subjects deserving of far greater detail.

Yet, for the general reader at least, one likes to think that the whole, consistently fascinating story of St Mary's is here — set down in a manner that should prove as enjoyable and entertaining to read as, in truth, it has been to write.

DON WALTER
HARROW ON THE HILL

## DEDICATION

For Will and Kate.

Archbishop Wulfred receives the Harrow lands in AD 825, as shown in
one of nine clerestory windows providing a pictorial history of St Mary's.

Its sheer comprehensiveness obviously impressed the populace. Although for a while it was called *The Book of the Treasury,* by the following century, it was commonly known by the far more awe-inspiring name of Domesday Book, Domesday being the day of the Last Judgement when all things are accountable.

It may also be useful to know that Middlesex was then divided for administrative purposes into six areas known as Hundreds. Harrow, together with Hendon, Kingsbury, Edgware and Stanmore, was in the Hundred of Gore, the latter being derived from the Saxon word *gara* meaning a triangular piece of land. The Hundred of Gore, of course, existed as a Petty Sessional Division right up to March 1986.

There are many books that give a clear breakdown of the social structure of the time: suffice it to say here that most of the county was divided into vills or manors, of which the latter generally consisted of two parts. There was the demesne (dominion) which the Lord of the Manor retained for his own support, the remainder of the Manor being held in villeinage — in other words, being parcelled out among the villeins and the cottagers who, in return gave service to the Manor's Lord, as required.

Serfdom still survived and, though today we would regard the serfs as slaves, their lives were at least under the protection of the law.

As Walter Druett and others have pointed out, each Manor was really like a miniature kingdom and, as such, wholly at the mercy of the Lord. In this context, Harrow could deem itself fortunate in its connection with Canterbury, for there is little doubt that the Archbishops exercised control without the extremes of cruelty and oppression practised by many lay Lords.

Domesday Book records the Lordship of Harrow as belonging to Archbishop Lanfranc. More excitingly for us, the Book also records the presence of a priest. Though no church is mentioned, he is shown to have one hide of land, a sizeable holding equalled by only two other priests in the whole of the county.

The rest of the local population is made up of three knights, with seven vassals, 102 villeins, two cottagers and two serfs, making a total of some 117 people. Most of those listed are likely to have been the heads of households holding land so the overall total can probably be trebled or even quadrupled. At 100 hides, the Harrow Manor was also the largest in Middlesex and its value was surpassed only by the Manors of Stepney, Fulham and Isleworth.

The Harrow of 1086 was thus a place of some size and importance — certainly, the most important community in the west of the county, which was otherwise sparsely populated.

Allowing for a few intelligent guesses, it is entirely possible to conjure up a plausible picture of this early community.

On the very top of the Hill (most likely where the Harrow School boarding house The Grove stands today) there would have been some kind of manor house occupied on occasion by the man who was both Archbishop and Lord of the Manor.

Nearby, we would find the respectable dwellings of the three knights and the seven vassals as well as a priest's house of an importance commensurate with his holding of land.

Scattered around the slopes of the hill there would be the many small tenements of the villeins and cottagers.

Elsewhere, we can envisage a landscape in which acres of arable land, hard-worked by men and oxen, is interspersed with forests of oak and beech sheltering the 2,000-odd swine that Domesday records within the Manor.

It would be a bold man who would positively assert that, in the most dominating position of all, we would see a church.

Yet, if there was a lack at the heart of this growing community, it was soon to be remedied, almost wholly due to the friendship of the Manor's Lord with the country's King.

Archbishop Lanfranc, founder of St Mary's in 1087 — from the stained glass window on the north side of the tower.

# LANFRANC AND THE FOUNDATION

Archbishop Lanfranc, who founded our St Mary's in 1087, was neither an Englishman nor a Norman but hailed from Pavia in Northern Italy, where he is said to have both taught and practised law.

The precise steps by which a Lombardian lawyer became England's Archbishop have been not so much lost in time as rooted in a legend concerning an encounter with robbers, interpreted as the spiritual turning point of his life.

As most frequently told, the story has the robbers stripping Lanfranc of his every possession and every garment except his cloak. Thinking perhaps to ingratiate himself with his attackers, he offered his cloak as well but, this being taken as mockery, he was beaten and tied to a tree. Suitably chastened, Lanfranc passed the hours in prayer until released by a fellow wayfarer. Asking the way to the nearest monastery, Lanfranc was then directed to the recently founded monastic house at Bec.

Here Lanfranc seems to have remained — and this much is factual — until 1063, when he was persuaded to become Abbot of St Stephen's at Caen.

Since St Stephen's was the personal foundation of William, Duke of Normandy, he quickly came to the attention of the future Conqueror of England and the two men forged a friendship which was to endure throughout their lives.

In his determination to be seen as a lawful monarch rather than a mere usurper, William had received the blessing of the Pope, Alexander II, even before his invasion of England. He had also won the support of Hildebrand, the influential Archdeacon of Rome who was to become Pope Gregory VII. Thus, and probably quite unwittingly, William had brought the Church in England to an entirely new stage in its development.

For the previous 500 years it had largely gone its own insular way. Now — and for the next 500 years — it would be more and more subject to the dictates of Rome.

Nevertheless, while accepting that the English Church must be brought into the mainstream of Continental church life, William was intent that his own leadership of the Church should remain unchallenged. It was therefore essential that his Archbishop of Canterbury should be a man in whom he could repose his complete personal trust.

There was, however, an immediate problem concerning the See of Canterbury. In the confused years prior to the Conquest, Edward the Confessor's Archbishop — the Norman Robert de Jumieges — had felt it politic to flee to his native Normandy. Although he had neither resigned the office nor been deposed from it, de Jumieges had long since been replaced by Archbishop Stigand.

Obviously there could be no place in Canterbury for Lanfranc while Stigand still held office so William now appealed to the Pope, knowing full well that the latter had never formally recognised Stigand's election. Just as William hoped, Stigand was promptly deposed and Lanfranc elected in his place.

Together, King and Archbishop now set about the task of reformation as they saw it. At first, they moved with caution, especially in such contentious issues as the celibacy of the clergy. Aware that the Pope desired a complete prohibition of clerical marriages, they nevertheless effected a compromise, allowing married clergy to retain their wives while debarring further married men from ordination.

More significantly, in view of the events that would come to a climax some 100 years later, they made moves to separate the ecclesiastical and civil courts. With the excuse that his foreign bishops were generally unacquainted with English law, William now ordered that the prelates should no longer adjudicate in combined courts. Instead, he appointed sheriffs and barons to judge civil affairs and declared that ecclesiastic matters should be brought before the higher clergy in ecclesiastical courts.

The chief result of this separation was to make it appear that the clergy was a distinct caste outside civil jurisdiction with the disastrous consequences we shall all too quickly discover.

Under Lanfranc, the English church also began to indulge a peculiarly Norman passion for building. At the same time that our St Mary's was rising on its special site — sometimes known as *Harrow-super-montem* — Canterbury Cathedral was also literally soaring from the ashes of the fire that had destroyed it in 1067. In truth, there was scarcely a parish church which was not rebuilt to the greater glory of God — and the greater dignity of England's new masters.

It is perhaps indicative of Lanfranc's wish to maintain a church apart from Rome that, although he travelled to Rome to accept his badge of office, the pallium, he went reluctantly — and never returned there.

This was entirely against the wishes of Pope Gregory VII who sought to compel periodic visits by representative prelates. It is still possible to read, often with mounting amusement, a whole sequence of letters in which the Archbishop offers — and the Pope rejects — increasingly weak excuses for his non-appearance in Rome.

By 1082, Gregory's patience was obviously close to exhaustion: 'The labour and difficulty of the journey is insufficient excuse for your absence' he wrote, 'when it is well known that many from a great distance — though weak and infirm of body and scarcely able to rise from their bed — have nevertheless out of their love of St Peter made haste to approach his threshold'.

Although King and Primate remained close, we can hardly assert that Lanfranc shared his monarch's secular pursuits but one surviving document certainly seems to nudge us in that direction. Addressed to Geoffrey de Mandeville, it reads as follows:-

'I hereby order and admonish you that the lands of Lanfranc the Archbishop which belongs to his Manor of Harrow you chase neither stags nor hind nor fallow deer nor hunt at all on them, except so far as he may order or permit'.

What gives this document added interest is that it was almost certainly addressed to de Mandeville not only in his official role as portreeve of London but also as Lanfranc's neighbour, Domesday Book listing him as the holder of the adjoining Manors of both Northolt and Greenford.

If this was indeed the case, it suggests that de Mandeville may well have been poaching on Lanfranc's land, possibly to such an extent that the Archbishop felt obliged to seek the King's intervention.

In any event, it adds another small human detail to a portrait that can still fascinate us 900 years on.

The Consecration by Anselm is depicted in another of the clerestory windows. Tradition claims that the Bishop of London tried to sabotage the ceremony.

17

Archbishop Anselm, later canonised as St Anselm, consecrated St Mary's
in 1094.

# ANSELM & THE CONSECRATION

Given that a period of seven years separates the foundation of St Mary's from its consecration, it is usually assumed that seven years was the time it took to build; indeed, this is not implausible when one considers the obvious difficulty of transporting every single block of stone to the top of the Hill by routes that can have been little more than cart-tracks.

Yet the possibility remains that the actual building was completed very much earlier and that a lengthy delay ensued simply because there was no Archbishop of Canterbury to carry out the task — and Canterbury, as we shall later see, was particularly anxious to retain the right of consecration.

The real problem was that the year that witnessed the foundation of St Mary's also saw the death of William the Conqueror, after an eleven-year reign so successful that the throne was able to pass to the son of his choice without dispute.

What William could not do, however, was to ensure that this second son, William II (variously known as William Rufus and William the Red), would be a truly worthy successor.

Even allowing for the fact that his subsequent battles with the Church did him no favours with the medieval chroniclers (who consequently painted him black as well as red) there can be no doubt that William Rufus was both weak and avaricious. Only 27 at his Coronation, he seems to have fallen into notably bad company, principally that of Ralph (Ranulf) Flambard, a name, as we shall see, with strong Harrow connections.

Flambard, described by the chronicler William of Malmesbury as 'a clergyman of the lowest origin but raised to eminence by his wit and subtlety' appears to have devised a singularly neat and simple way of robbing the Church. Whenever a vacancy occurred in a bishopric, the income was promptly appropriated by the Crown. Since it was the King who normally appointed the Bishops, vacancies could, in theory, stretch into infinity.

Not even Canterbury escaped his clutches. Lanfranc barely outlived the King, dying in 1089, yet four years later, no successor had been appointed.

Then William Rufus fell seriously ill. In a notably superstitious age, William seems to have interpreted his illness as a sign of God's displeasure, in which case his recovery might well depend on the speedy appointment of an Archbishop.

There was really only one candidate — Anselm, renowned as the holiest man in Europe; also, the man who, some 30 years earlier, had succeeded Lanfranc as Prior of Bec.

Anselm, in fact, was no stranger to England. He had previously visited his old friend, the ailing Earl of Chester. He is also reputed to have inspected his Abbey's properties in England, which would likely have meant a visit to the Manor of Ruislip, which William I had granted to the Benedictines in 1087.

Much of our authority for these and subsequent events comes from the writings of the man known as the Good Monk Eadmer, whom Done Bushell has tellingly described as a Boswell to Anselm's Dr Johnson.

Eadmer who, from early childhood, had been raised in the monastery of Christ Church, Canterbury, first made Anselm's acquaintance as early as 1071 and the two men remained life-long friends and companions.

From Eadmer we learn that Anselm was wholly reluctant to accept the Primacy.

First, he doubted that the King was truly sick unto death; then he offered excuse after excuse. He was too old (he was, in fact, about 60). He had no stomach for administration. He could not leave his Abbey.

When it seemed certain that Anselm could not be persuaded by normal means, it is said the Archbishop's crozier was literally forced into his hands, whereupon he is supposed to have thrust his hands deep into his pockets. The bishops then allegedly grabbed his arms and forced his fingers apart so that he had no option but to grasp the crozier.

Later, Anselm himself was to describe the scene in a letter to his monks at Bec: 'It would have been difficult to make out whether madmen were dragging along one in his senses', he wrote 'or sane men, a madman'. Elsewhere, he referred to himself as an old and feeble sheep yoked to an untameable bull — and so, indeed, it proved.

Anselm's consecration as Primate took place in December 1093 which was only a mere month before he, in turn, was to consecrate the new church dedicated to the Virgin Mother at Harrow.

The service at St Mary's was therefore his first consecration in England. It also associates us with the first of his many battles with the King.

Eadmer dates the occasion precisely, writing that Anselm 'presented himself at the royal court at Christmas time'. The first three days of the Feast apparently passed pleasantly enough but then, according to Eadmer, 'the King's mind was turned against him . . . because he refused to despoil his tenants in order to give the King the equivalent of £1,000 as a thank offering for his munificence'.

It appeared that Anselm had originally offered the equivalent of £500 but, when double that sum was demanded, he had deemed it politic to give the original £500 to the poor.

It would be nice to think that some of it came the way of the poor of Harrow for, in Eadmer's own words, 'having angered his lord, he left the court . . . and went to his village at Harrow'.

Done Bushell vividly imagines the pleasure Anselm would have found in the tranquillity of the Hill. 'It must have been like Bec to him', he writes. Nevertheless, Anselm's stay at Harrow was not without a note of drama.

Around this time, Anselm received a letter from Maurice, Bishop of London, protesting that, since Harrow was in his London diocese, it was his responsibility to consecrate the church.

Though Anselm was convinced he had the right of consecration in what was, after all, his own Manor, he tactfully referred the matter to Wulfstan, the one surviving Saxon bishop and a wise old man of 85. In his wisdom — or was it perhaps more a matter of diplomacy? — Wulfstan ruled in favour of the senior prelate.

This should have been the end of the matter, but on the consecration day in January 1094, just two days before Old Christmas Day, representatives of the Bishop of London arrived at Harrow determined to prevent the ceremony by any means, however unscrupulous. In the event, it seems that a clerk in their pay smuggled himself into the company of the Archbishop's clerks and, just before the ceremony began, stole the episcopal chrismatory and made off into the crowd.

Just what happened next we shall never know but the thief appears to have been stopped by the crowd and the stolen vessel recovered in time for the ceremony to proceed. The normally reliable Eadmer, however, adds a few embellishments of his own, possibly to emphasise the holiness of Anselm.

Since his near-miraculous tale has been displayed in St Mary's (near the south porch door) for as long as the writer can remember, we need have no hesitation in repeating at least a small section of it.

According to the Eadmer version, the thief was going along the road to London with his stolen property when he turned back, thinking that he had taken a wrong direction.

But, even after retracing his steps, it still seemed to him that he was going back to the place from which he was running away. As Eadmer relates, 'This happened several times and he wandered and strayed here and there, not knowing where he was going, so that the people who saw him behaving like this wondered what was the matter'. His behaviour was so suspicious, in fact, that the thief was ultimately stopped and the stolen vessel found beneath his cloak.

Eadmer, however, cannot resist a final twist to the tale in which the Archbishop orders the clerk to be set free and return home.

'As soon as he was free', Eadmer informs us, 'he went off without hesitation along the road which he had been quite unable to keep to when burdened with his theft'.

In the years that followed St Mary's consecration, Anselm continued to clash with his King, not least over the monarch's steadfast refusal to allow him to receive the pallium in Rome. Anselm finally travelled to the Vatican under his own authority — in effect, going into voluntary exile, where he remained until William Rufus was killed by an arrow while hunting in the New Forest.

Although some now argue that the alleged accident had been engineered by William's brother and successor, Henry I, the latter certainly proved to be the better King. Nevertheless, relations between Church and Crown were no more harmonious than before, especially as Anselm's exile had allied him even more strongly with Rome.

The conflict was still very much alive at Anselm's death in 1107 and was, as we shall see, to be renewed even more fiercely just a few decades later.

Within a few decades of Becket's last visit, St Mary's acquired its beautiful
Purbeck marble font.

# THE YOUNG BECKET

Possibly because his story has been told and re-told in so many dramatic works of the 20th century, Thomas Becket seems to be far more accessible to us — in time as well as in personality — than Anselm, yet only a dozen or more years separates Anselm's death from Becket's birth. (This is equally true whether we accept 1118 as Becket's birthdate or, as some historians have it, 1120).

In all other respects, there seems very little that we do not know about Becket since, by the manner of his life — and, even more, by the manner of his death — he was a favourite subject for the medieval chroniclers.

One of the most vivid of these near-contemporary writers, to whom we shall be constantly turning, is William FitzStephen who, in his *Life of St Thomas* carefully sets out his own credentials:

'I was a witness of his passion at Canterbury', he writes, 'and many other things which are here written I saw with my own eyes and heard with my ears'. Though he admits that 'others I learned from those who were cognisant of them', his testimony is about as good as we can expect of events that happened well over 800 years ago.

Even if some doubt still clings to the actual year, we know that Becket was born at his father's house in Cheapside, London, on 21 December and that he was baptised in St Mary Cole Church. Gilbert, his father, was a Norman, believed to have been a native of Rouen, while his mother came from Caen. By the time of Becket's birth, FitzStephen tells us, they had become citizens of London — 'of the middle class, not making money by usury nor engaged in business but living respectably on their income'. In fact, Gilbert later became Sheriff of London and young Thomas was sent to study in Paris.

Though a degree of permissible flattery may be allowed his chroniclers, Becket genuinely seems to have been a handsome youth 'tall of stature with a prominent and slightly aquiline nose, nimble and active in his movements, gifted with eloquence of speech and an acute intelligence'; indeed, all he lacked for the highest advancement was nobility of birth.

From a comparatively early age it must have been apparent that only the Church could provide a route to high office yet, initially at least, Becket seems to have shown little interest in theological study. Instead, on leaving school where he had attained considerable fluency in Latin, he worked as a clerk and accountant to the sheriffs.

'As his years and virtues increased' — as FitzStephen nicely puts it — Becket was enabled, in 1143, to enter the service of Theobald, Archbishop of Canterbury, in part through the good offices of his father who had once been a neighbour of the Archbishop in Normandy.

What makes the introduction especially relevant to our narrative is that, according to FitzStephen, young Becket 'first came to the Archbishop's court at the town of Harrow'.

Furthermore, if FitzStephen is to be believed, Harrow also provided the background for one of those near-miraculous incidents that invariably enliven the early lives of those we have come to regard as saints. In this instance, it seems that Becket and his companion, a Norman gentleman-at-arms called Ralph Baille-Hache, were lodged at a Harrow inn.

But let FitzStephen continue the narrative: 'On the night of his arrival his hostess dreamed a dream in which she saw him seated on the roof of the church whilst from it his robes hung down and covered the whole edifice. On the morrow she told her husband of her dream and put upon it the interpretation that one of the young men (for as yet she knew not whither of the two was Thomas) would be hereafter ruler of the church pertaining to the Manor'.

On a more factual basis, Becket's journey to Archbishop Theobald at Harrow does have the feeling of a turning point in a previously unsettled life and one can readily understand Done Bushell's remark that the Harrow tower (there was, of course, no spire at that time) must have represented 'visibly and outwardly a most momentous choice'.

In 1143, when he held court at Harrow, Theobald had been Archbishop for only five years during which the Pope had made persistent efforts to establish a spiritual supremacy over the Church in England. (In this, Rome had been greatly helped by the attitude of Theobald's predecessor, William de Corbeuil, who is said to have regarded himself as the Pope's deputy in England). Theobald's court had nevertheless become a focal point for the finest minds and talents in the realm and there could have been no better patron — or more rewarding environment — for a young man of Becket's abilities and ambitions.

The first preferments quickly followed; first, Becket became rector of the church of St Mary Le Strand and, then, the church of Otford in Kent.

As FitzStephen records, 'in process of time and as a regard for his merits, the Archbishop . . . made him deacon of Canterbury'. This in itself was no mean achievement, being regarded as the most dignified office in the English Church after the bishops and abbots; moreover, it was 'worth to him a hundred pounds of silver'.

In October 1154, King Stephen died at Canterbury and, within months, Theobald was called upon to crown his successor, Henry of Anjou, a grandson of Henry I.

Henry II was young (only 21 at his Coronation) and many of those in his immediate circle were known to dislike the Church. According to the contemporary writer Roger of Pontigny, Theobald felt that it would be a shrewd political move to have a churchman close to the throne so, around January 1155, Thomas Becket found himself translated from the court of the Archbishop to that of the King.

Soon he was Thomas the Chancellor, a title he used in many of the various charters that still survive.

If anything, Theobald's plan worked only too well and the two men — King and Chancellor — soon became the closest of friends. Becket was some 14 or so years older than his monarch, nevertheless, according to Pontigny, the King 'lavished upon him such great affection as one may think he had never bestowed on any man before'.

FitzStephen also tells us that 'when the daily round of business had been dealt with, the King and Thomas would sport together like boys of the same age, in hall, in church, and while sitting or riding abroad'.

That it was the kind of over-excited play that, in younger children, leads to bedtime tears is amply demonstrated in many of the stories that have been handed down to us, of which the most vivid is the oft-repeated tale of the Chancellor's cloak.

Apparently, the two men were out riding in the hard winter weather when they came across a poor man in a thin and ragged coat. The King declared it would be an act of charity to give him a thick warm cloak but it was obviously Becket's cloak he had in mind; indeed, after some spirited horseplay, he managed to pull it from his Chancellor's shoulders and press it upon the astonished peasant.

In truth, in richness of apparel there was rarely little to choose between the two and it seems to have been the unsuitability of his clothing that immediately sprang to Becket's mind when, some seven years later, the King made a momentous — and, as it proved, calamitous — decision.

At the time the two men were at the King's castle of Falaise in Normandy. Becket was about to depart for England on Royal business when Henry suddenly announced that he wished his friend to succeed the recently deceased Archbishop Theobald.

Thomas Becket is known to have made at least three visits to St Mary's.

According to Herbert of Bosham, a close friend and possibly an eye-witness to the whole exchange, Becket professed to take the suggestion as a joke. Pointing to his lavish attire, he mockingly remarked 'How religious, how saintly is the man you would appoint to that holy see and over so renowned and pious a body of men'.

Roger de Pontigny claims that Thomas Becket opposed the King's plan by every means in his power — but to no avail and on 3 June 1162, he was duly consecrated Archbishop of Canterbury.

Two of his very first actions as Primate of England proved to have lasting consequences.

First, to mark the day of his translation to the Primacy, he instituted the Festival of Trinity Sunday, the observance of which was later extended to the whole Western Church.

Shortly afterwards, though the date is uncertain, Becket relinquished the secular duties of the Chancellor.

This, in itself, was greatly vexatious to the King who had always anticipated having the man he had hitherto called his friend in both vital roles. This disagreement, however, was as nothing compared to the gulf that was shortly and disastrously to open between them.

25

The external arch to the west door still bears some of its original Norman
ornamentation. The door, too, is of great antiquity.

# ROAD TO MARTYRDOM

It would be easy to say that Thomas the Archbishop was a very different man from Thomas the Chancellor but it seems more likely that the assumption of his new role brought to the fore characteristics that were already present in his make-up, not least a genuine piety. In fact, we are told that, even throughout his years as Chancellor, Thomas had often received discipline in private, 'baring his back to the lash'.

Certainly, from the moment he assumed the Primacy, he realised the impossibility of serving two masters whose demands were so much at variance.

At first, his disagreements with the King were relatively trivial but, very soon, a much more serious conflict over clerical immunities began to emerge.

Even if this writer could claim the knowledge, this is not the place to discuss in any depth the rival claims of civil law and canon law.

There was, however, such an ill-defined overlap between the two that some sort of clash was inevitable, given the determination of the King to reclaim the prerogative of the Crown in such matters, which he felt had been diminished under his immediate predecessor, King Stephen.

In particular, he wished to be assured that there would be no repetition of earlier scandals involving clerks in holy orders. Even though manifestly guilty of serious crimes, many had escaped sentence — or received ludicrously light sentences — on being tried in the canon court.

In October 1163 King Henry convened a great council at Westminster to determine the matter.

His intention was that any clergy convicted in the spiritual courts of such major crimes as murder or robbery should be delivered up to the officers of the Royal courts to be dealt with according to the law of the land. It seems that he put his case with some conviction and was likely to have won the bishops' assent but for the vehemence and eloquence with which Becket spoke against him.

Having written to Pope Alexander III for advice, Becket now retired to his Harrow Manor to await a reply. As Done Bushell has written: 'We cannot doubt that as the Archbishop offered day by day the holy Scripture in Harrow Church, it was with prayers that . . . he might at least receive from Rome a full and generous support'.

Three Papal messengers, led by Philip, Abbot of L'Aumone did, indeed, arrive in Harrow but their message urged not resistance but submission to the King (whom the Pope had no particular wish to offend).

This time Becket had no option but to obey but never again was he to be so submissive. During the following months, the two men constantly clashed, most notably over the Constitution of Clarendon, which had the primary objective of making the clergy amenable to the civil courts.

By the following year, (1164), the relationship had so deteriorated that, at the Council of Northampton, Becket was accused of contempt of the Crown and condemned to forfeit all his goods and moveables at the King's mercy.

The Archbishop now felt it wise to flee the country and appeal in person to the Pope, then in exile in France following the occupation of the Vatican by the Emperor Frederick Barbarossa. Henry also despatched envoys both to the Pope and to the French King, Louis VII.

Henry's arguments, however, fell on less than sympathetic ears for King Louis, as a devout son of the Church, was amazed at the audacity of Henry's letter in referring to Becket as 'formerly Archbishop of Canterbury'.

Becket, on the other hand, acted with considerable political guile by literally resigning the Archbishopric into the hands of the Pope. Some sources even state that he handed the Pope the archiepiscopal ring.

As Becket must surely have anticipated, the Pope insisted on reinstating both office and ring and henceforth Becket was able to claim that he held the Primacy not from the King but from the Pope himself; also, at the Pope's suggestion, he entered the Cistercian Abbey of Pontigny.

At this juncture, however, the Pope was unwilling to commit himself wholly to Becket's cause, being reluctant to lose the support of England in his struggle with Barbarossa, who had by now installed the so-called Anti-Pope, Victor IV. Instead, he counselled moderation, stating that 'many things must be endured because of the times'.

Undeterred, Becket continued to write the King letters which even a less choleric man than Henry would have considered inflammatory. 'In that you are my king', one typical letter declared, 'I am bound to you in reverence and regard; in that you are my spiritual son, I am bound by reason of my office to chasten and correct you'.

When no replies of any kind were forthcoming, Becket chose Whit Sunday 1166, on which to excommunicate all those he regarded as his enemies. Yet he still could not bring himself to pass sentence on the King, especially after news had been brought that Henry had fallen ill.

Becket remained at Pontigny until November 1166 when a threat to confiscate all the property of the Cistercians in England caused him to seek shelter with King Louis at Sens.

Over the next four years, no fewer than three separate legations were appointed in an attempt to bring about a reconciliation. Nevertheless the year 1170 brought only new cause for strife when the King determined to crown his elder son, Young Henry.

In protecting the succession, Henry was merely following the custom of other Royal houses but, understandably, Becket chose to interpret the King's decision as the cruellest of personal blows. As Archbishop he argued it was his traditional right to perform the Coronation; also, in happier times, he had been charged with the boy's education.

Henry seems to have intended that the Archbishop of York should perform the ceremony but, in February 1170, a Papal Bull was issued informing the English Bishops that 'if any of you shall dare to act with such presumption . . . the deed will redound to the peril of his order and his office'.

Whether this warning was actually delivered (and there is some doubt in the matter), Henry went ahead with his plans.

As it proved, he could hardly have made a greater mistake. Not only did the Coronation offend the Pope, it also angered King Louis because the ceremony had been performed without the presence of Margaret, his daughter, who many years before had been given in marriage to Young Henry. (Ironically, it had been Becket who, as Chancellor, had once carried out the delicate marriage negotiations).

Alarmed that everyone had now turned against him, King Henry agreed to meet with Becket at Freteval.

In another of his fascinating eye-witness accounts, Henry of Bosham tells us how Becket dismounted from his horse and 'humbly prostrated himself at the King's feet' whereupon the King had held the stirrup for the Archbishop to remount. At this highly emotional moment, both men were undoubtedly sincere in reaffirming their friendship. There were, however, too many other factors at work to allow them to pursue any genuinely personal solution to their problems.

Although the King summoned Becket to return to England, neither man's behaviour was notable for its temperance in the days that followed.

First, Henry decided to remain in France himself; then, Becket was provided with an entirely unsuitable escort in the person of an old enemy, the Dean of Salisbury, whom he had excommunicated some years before.

For his part, Becket's last action on French soil on 30 November 1170, was to dispatch letters suspending the Archbishop of York (who had, indeed, performed Young Henry's Coronation) and excommunicating afresh the Bishops of London and Salisbury.

Becket received a tumultuous reception on his return to Canterbury. Thus encouraged, he sent a message to the Young King intimating that he wished to pay his respects in person. He had, moreover, brought the boy a valuable charger for, as FitzStephen reminds us, 'he had a real affection for the lad whom he had brought up in his own court and household'.

Becket's journey to the Palace at Woodstock in Oxfordshire quickly turned into something of a triumphal cavalcade but, at Southwark on 11 December, it was halted by a message from the Young King declaring that the Archbishop was not permitted to visit him nor allowed to enter the cities and castles of the realm. The message continued: 'Let him rather return to Canterbury and remain in his see'.

This sudden change of heart seems to have been provoked by Becket's enemies, who falsely reported that the Archbishop's triumphant but essentially peaceful progress through the countryside was that of a man 'careering about the kingdom at the head of a strong force of armed men'.

Rather than face the return journey to Canterbury, Becket decided to go straight to his Manor House at Harrow, where he arrived on or about St Lucy Day, Sunday 13 December 1170.

There were, in fact, very good reasons for coming to Harrow at that time.

First, there was the simple matter of convenience. The Harrow Manor was near to Southwark, where his procession had been halted. It was also relatively close to St Albans and his old friend and confidant Abbot Simon.

But there may well have been a deeper underlying motive.

The Rector of Harrow since 1163 had been Nigel de Sackville, usually referred to as 'the usurping Rector' since he had been appointed by the King in the Archbishop's absence. Not surprisingly, Becket seems to have taken de Sackville's intrusion as a personal insult.

He may therefore have wanted to reassert his full authority in a place which had been of very special significance to him since the days of his mentor, Theobald.

Becket's contemporary biographers tend to omit the events of 11-17 December but, happily for us, they are fully covered in the later narrative of Matthew Paris, chief copyist at St Albans Abbey.

Matthew Paris tells us Becket regarded the Abbot as 'a very ready and helpful comforter, above all others' so it is entirely in character that Abbot Simon should not only travel to Harrow but should then offer to journey to Woodstock to intercede for him at the Young King's court. Done Bushell assesses the Harrow to Woodstock journey as a long day's ride so we can assume that the Abbot's mission occupied the three days of 14-16 December.

At Woodstock, Paris tells us the Abbot was given a decidedly stormy reception: 'There were some who clenched their fists' he writes, 'and others who half drew their knives, all swearing horribly that but for a very little barrier hindered them from disembowelling, or even worse, the messenger who came from so pronounced a traitor.'

It is all too easy to imagine the sadness of the Abbot's return to Harrow, with Christmas only days away. As the two men bade farewell — for what was to prove to be the last time — Becket announced his intention of returning to Canterbury and keeping 'in the Church entrusted to my care such Festival as God may there provide'.

29

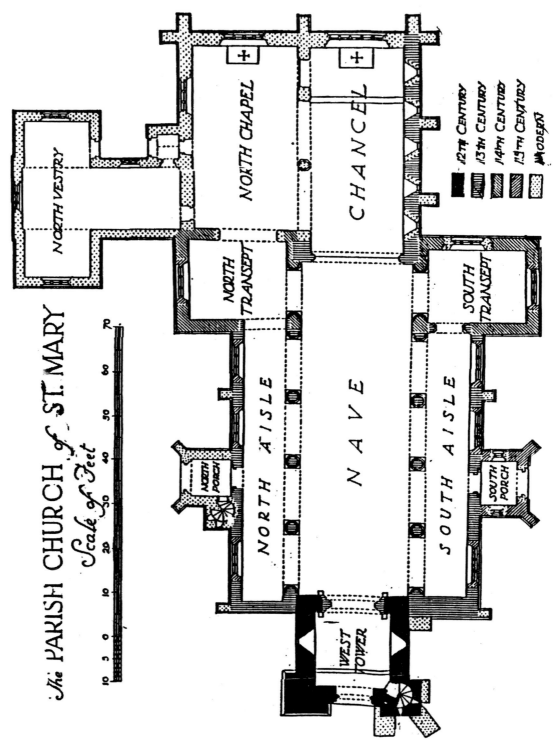

The PARISH CHURCH of ST. MARY
Scale of Feet

NORTH VESTRY

NORTH CHAPEL

CHANCEL

12TH CENTURY
13TH CENTURY
14TH CENTURY
15TH CENTURY
MODERN

NORTH TRANSEPT

SOUTH TRANSEPT

NORTH AISLE

NAVE

SOUTH AISLE

NORTH PORCH

SOUTH PORCH

WEST TOWER

As this date-plan reveals, today's St Mary's is a mix of many different periods and architectural styles.

30

Becket did, indeed, celebrate the Feast in his own cathedral but, even at this time and this place, he could not find it in his heart to forgive his enemies. Instead, as the contemporary Ralph de Diceto tells us: 'He ascended to the pulpit on Christmas Day . . . and when the sermon was ended solemnly excommunicated Nigel de Sackville who had by violence seized up the Church of Harrow . . . and Robert de Broc who had of insult and contempt cut off the tail of one of the Archbishop's sumpter horses'.

This last (and somewhat bathetic) detail has, over the years, given rise to all kinds of local legends, the most dramatic of which has de Broc and his men firing arrows at the departing Becket and his retinue from the tower of St Mary's.

The truth is probably as mundane as de Diceto suggests — someone, possibly de Broc's nephew, John, may well have spitefully mutilated a horse in Becket's retinue. In any event, the de Broc family were soon to be implicated in a far more heinous crime.

It sprang, in fact, from a meeting in France between the King (who had remained out of the country throughout these recent events) and the Archbishop of York and the Bishops of London and Salisbury who had no doubt crossed the Channel intent on revenge. According to FitzStephen, they assured the King that 'while Thomas lives, you will have neither peace nor quiet nor see good days'.

Whatever the King's exact response (and 'Who will rid me of this turbulent priest?' is almost certainly a latter-day invention), it was couched in sufficiently angry terms for four knights of the Royal household to interpret it as a call to murder.

The four — Reginald FitzUrse, William de Traci, Hugh of Morville and Richard Britto — promptly sailed for England. Though they left from different ports, their destination was the same — the de Broc castle at Saltwood near Hythe. Here they gathered a small force of armed men — Robert de Broc among them — and marched to Canterbury, arriving on Tuesday 29 December. After thrusting their way into the Cathedral, the knights made some attempt to force Becket to utter words of submission but, in truth, there could be only one outcome.

Thus, in the dim late afternoon light of the Cathedral, the Archbishop was mortally wounded by four massive sword blows.

When it was thought that the murderers, mindful of the consequences of their sacrilege, would drag the body outside, the monks hastily interred it in the crypt. Becket's body, in fact, remained in the crypt until July 1220, when it was removed to that special shrine which figures later in our story — again with a strong and shameful Harrow connection.

There is no doubt that Henry was devastated by the news of Becket's death though one has leave to doubt whether this was as much from personal sorrow as a realisation that, in his battle with the Church, he was quite clearly the loser.

Henry might well have expected personal excommunication and his lands to be placed under interdict; instead, after much negotiation, he was permitted to swear a solemn oath exculpating himself from complicity in the murder. The Pope, however, exacted a considerable price for his leniency in terms of men and resources required to fight the infidel.

Finally, some four years after the murder, Henry made his now celebrated act of penance when, at the Canterbury tomb of the recently canonised St Thomas of Canterbury, he allowed himself to be scourged by the monks.

As for Thomas Becket, it has to be said that few men have ever achieved so speedily so great a posthumous fame. But then few men have ever lived such a life — or died such a death.

By the year 1200 no fewer than nine biographies had appeared in Latin and one in French, of which three were the work of men who had actually been present at his martyrdom.

By the late Middle Ages the youth who had once travelled to Harrow, possibly unsure of his Christian vocation, had become incontrovertibly the most popular saint in Western Christendom.

# Archbishops of Canterbury

#### who were

# Lords of the Manor of Harrow.

### A.D. 825 to A.D. 1545.

| | Name | Description | A.D. |
|---|---|---|---|
| Coins | WULFRED | ... | 805 to 832 |
| | FEOLOGILD | ... | 832 |
| Coins | CEOLNOTH | ... | 833 to 870 |
| Coin | ETHELRED | He sent a Mission to the Christians of India in 888. | 870 to 889 |
| | PLEGMUND | ... | 870 to 914 |
| | ATHELM | ... | 914 to 923 |
| | WULFHELM | ... | 923 to 942 |
| | ODO | ... | 942 to 959 |
| Portrait | DUNSTAN | ... | 960 to 988 |
| | ETHELGAR | ... | 988 to 989 |
| | SIGERIC | ... | 990 to 994 |
| | ÆLFRIC | ... | 995 to 1005 |
| Portrait | AELFHEAH (S. ALPHEGE) | ... | 1005 to 1012 |
| | LYFING | ... | 1013 to 1020 |
| | AETHELNOTH | ... | 1020 to 1038 |
| | EADSIGE | ... | 1038 to 1050 |
| | ROBERT | ... | 1051 to 1052 |
| Portrait | STIGAND | ... | 1052 to 1070 |
| | LANFRANC | ... | 1070 to 1089 |
| Portrait | ANSELM | ... | 1093 to 1109 |
| Seal | RALPH D'ESCURES | ... | 1114 to 1122 |
| Seal | WILLIAM DE CORBEUIL | ... | 1123 to 1136 |
| Seal | THEOBALD | ... | 1138 to 1161 |
| Portrait and Seals | THOMAS BECKET | Lord Chancellor. | 1162 to 1170 |

| | Name | Description | A.D. |
|---|---|---|---|
| Seal | RICHARD | ... | 1174 to 1181 |
| Seal | BALDWIN | He died in the Holy Land. | 1185 to 1190 |
| Tomb | HUBERT WALTER | Justiciar and Lord Chancellor. He accompanied Richard I. to the Holy Land. | 1193 to 1205 |
| Tomb and Seal | STEPHEN LANGTON | Cardinal. His Constitutions were issued in 1222. | 1207 to 1228 |
| Seal | RICHARD LE GRANT, also called RICHARD OF WETHERSHED. | | 1229 to 1231 |
| Seal | EDMUND RICH OF ABINGDON | His Constitutions were issued in 1236. | 1234 to 1240 |
| Portrait and Seal | BONIFACE OF SAVOY | | 1241 to 1270 |
| Seal | ROBERT KILWARDBY | ... | 1272 to 1278 |
| Tomb | JOHN PECKHAM | ... | 1279 to 1292 |
| Seal | ROBERT WINCHELSEY | ... | 1294 to 1313 |
| Tomb | WALTER REYNOLDS | Lord Treasurer, Lord Chancellor. | 1313 to 1327 |
| Tomb | SIMON MEPEHAM | ... | 1328 to 1333 |
| Tomb | JOHN STRATFORD | Lord Chancellor. | 1333 to 1348 |
| | THOMAS BRADWARDINE | He died of the Black Death. | 1349 |
| Seal | SIMON ISLIP | ... | 1349 to 1366 |
| Portrait | SIMON LANGHAM | Lord Treasurer, Lord Chancellor, Cardinal. | 1366 to 1368 |
| | WILLIAM WHITTLESEY | ... | 1368 to 1374 |

| | Name | Description | A.D. |
|---|---|---|---|
| Tomb | SIMON SUDBURY | Lord Chancellor. He cited Wyclif in 1378, and was beheaded by the Wat Tyler Rebels at the instance of John Ball. | 1375 to 1381 |
| Tomb | WILLIAM COURTENAY | ... | 1381 to 1396 |
| Portrait | THOMAS ARUNDEL | Lord Chancellor. | (1396 to 1398 / (1399 to 1414 |
| | ROGER WALDEN | Lord Treasurer. | 1398 |
| Portrait and Tomb | HENRY CHICHELEY | He founded All Souls College, Oxford, in 1437; and it is recorded on the Court Rolls of the Manor of Harrow in 1445 that "the woods were grievously "devastated by reason of the timber having been "felled for the building of the College of the Lord "Henry Chichele, the late Archbishop, at Oxford." | 1414 to 1443 |
| Seal | JOHN STAFFORD | Keeper of the Privy Seal, Lord Treasurer, Lord Chancellor. | 1443 to 1452 |
| Tomb | JOHN KEMP | Keeper of the Privy Seal, Lord Chancellor, Cardinal. | 1452 to 1454 |
| Tomb | THOMAS BOURCHIER | Lord Chancellor, Cardinal. | 1454 to 1486 |
| Tomb | JOHN MORTON | Lord Chancellor, Cardinal. | 1486 to 1500 |
| | HENRY DEAN | Master in Chancery, Lord Keeper of the Great Seal. | 1501 to 1503 |
| Portrait | WILLIAM WARHAM | Master of the Rolls, Lord Keeper of the Great Seal, Lord Chancellor. | 1503 to 1532 |
| Portrait | THOMAS CRANMER | He surrendered the Manor of Harrow to the Crown in 1545. | 1533 to 1556 |

Listed here are the successive Archbishops of Canterbury who held the Lordship of Harrow for over eight centuries.

32

# THE FIRST REBUILDING

Attractive as the notion is, it would be mistaken to assume that the church in which Becket preached was fundamentally the same as the church we know today.

Admittedly, the cruciform ground plan would be very little different from that of today but there can be no ignoring the fact that our contemporary St Mary's provides visible evidence of at least two re-buildings even before Gilbert Scott's major 19th century restoration.

According to Samuel Gardner, who wrote a widely admired *Architectural History of the Church* about 100 years ago, the first re-building probably started around the year 1200, at a time when the life of the community totally revolved around the parish church.

In Harrow, as elsewhere throughout the country, there were thus compelling reasons for rebuilding. In Gardner's view, the fabric of St Mary's may still be the same as Lanfranc's original church 'to a height of a foot or two above floor level' but, some 100 years after the consecration, he believes a reconstruction took place. All the technical evidence seems to point to this work involving the complete rebuilding of the chancel and south transept and the commencement of a new nave; however, Gardner, in common with other experts, is convinced that there was a long break between the start of this work and its completion.

He hazards a guess that problems of settlement might have frightened the builders and caused a stoppage 'until larger stones and more skilled workmen could be obtained'.

There are, however, even more convincing historical reasons for the delay, not least the fact that, for some 30 years (roughly 1189-1219) England was notably unlucky in its kings.

First, there was Richard I who, for all his popular lion-hearted image, was far more interested in the Crusades than in events in his own country, in which he seems to have spent only some 4-5 months throughout his entire reign.

Next, there was his brother John, who cruelly allowed his people to be the real victims of a dispute with Pope Innocent III.

The trouble all began with the death in 1205 of Archbishop Hubert Walter. Within days of his demise the monks of Canterbury had not only chosen their own sub-prior Reginald to be the next Primate of England but had also despatched him to Rome to obtain his pall. King John, however, had his own candidate in John de Grey, Bishop of Norwich, who was both his secretary and personal friend.

Predictably, both parties appealed to the Pope whose somewhat drastic solution was to elect a third man. His choice was Stephen Langton, then lecturing in theology at the Curia and undoubtedly the most suitable candidate of the three.

King John, however, refused to allow Langton even to set foot in England and, like Anselm and Becket before him, Archbishop Stephen Langton was obliged to remain in exile. Even more incredibly, this state of affairs was allowed to continue for some three years by which time an infuriated Pope was ready to use his most powerful weapon.

Accordingly, in March 1208, he placed the whole of England under an Interdict which effectively meant that the whole land was to be treated as abhorrent to and forsaken of God.

Churches were to be closed; there were to be no church ceremonies except the baptism of infants and the confessions of the dying; even the dead were to be buried in unconsecrated ground.

For John, who rarely entered a place of worship when it was open, the closure of the churches was hardly a matter of consequence but there is no doubt that the Interdict fell heavily upon the poor and the devout; indeed, it has been said that many never subsequently recovered the habit of public worship.

33

The Pope's action also provided John with the perfect excuse to confiscate the goods of the clergy. At Harrow, for example, the Archiepiscopal Manor was given to two of the King's cronies, Peter de Crohun and Eudo de Lascelles.

The Pope now ordered John's excommunication. When this brought the monarch no nearer to submission, Innocent III proposed that John be deposed in favour of King Philip of France, who had but recently conquered Normandy. Philip was already making plans for England's invasion when King John gave way.

The full circumstances that ultimately brought about the lifting of the Interdict in 1214 are not truly part of this narrative; nevertheless it is worth recording that, when John received his kingdom back, it was as an acknowledged vassal of the Pope to whom he was to pay an annual sum in tribute.

Against such a background, it may seem surprising that the first clause of the Magna Carta (the great charter of English civil and political liberties John was obliged to sign in 1215) was that 'the Church of England be free'. There is little doubt, however, that the original meaning was that it should be free from Royal interference and thus free to obey the ecclesiastical authority of Rome.

At this date we can never know the impact of the Interdict on the Church at Harrow (and certainly many commentators feel that its effects have been overstated). Nevertheless it is surely significant that the well-authenticated gap in the rebuilding of St Mary's coincided so neatly with this grievously troubled time.

Even allowing for modern techniques and scholarship, there are still difficulties in dating accurately the fabric of a church. Daniel Lysons' famous 1795 publication, *The Environs of London* can be forgiven for falling into several understandable traps.

For example, the fact that the early 13th century rebuilders almost certainly modelled the columns of the nave arcade on their massive Norman predecessors persuaded Lysons to consider them part of Lanfranc's original church.

Lysons also claimed that the present font was as old as the church itself. Given its general design and material (Purbeck marble) current scholarship more convincingly ascribes it to a date around the end of the 12th or beginning of the 13th century. Nevertheless one can still legitimately thrill to the thought that this modestly beautiful piece in which today's generation is baptised was already in place — and in use — when the first rebuilding began.

A staircase of comparatively recent origin leads to the parvise, the little room above the south porch, possibly the site of the original chantry chapel.

Part of the actual endowment of the Vicarage, which dates from around 1234-40, listing all the tithes, including little pigs, goats and bees.

# THE VICARAGE ENDOWED

Whatever else it achieved, the greater authority now exercised by the Pope in English ecclesiastical affairs almost certainly paved the way for the endowment of our Harrow Vicarage.

Certainly, in 1215, Pope Innocent III conducted a survey of the Church which convinced him that educated men in England would only serve as parish priests if they were given a reasonable living and some security of tenure. As a direct result, he instructed his diocesan bishops to institute vicarages throughout the country.

The exact date of the endowment at Harrow is unclear but, in his 19th century researches, Done Bushell unearthed at the Library of Lambeth Palace a confirmation by Archbishop Courtenay dated April 1396 of letters by Edmund Rich, one of his predecessors. These admitted one John de Holtune as Vicar of Harrow on the Hill on the presentation of Master Elias de Dereham.

Since Rich was Primate of England from 1234-40 the vicarage was presumably endowed some time during that seven-year period.

The Deed of Endowment lists all the offerings that were to be made to the Vicar and thus provides a fascinating glimpse of what was obviously a highly agricultural community. Among other offerings, for example, were all the tithes of lambs, wool, cheese, butter, milk, chickens, calves, little pigs, goats and bees of the Lord Archbishop and the parishioners; also the tithes of hay of Hamo and Hugh de Rokeseie (at Roxeth) and of Ailwin de la Hegge (at Headstone); also the whole tithe of the pannage (beechnuts, acorns etc) of the Lord Archbishop, and the tithe of flax, hemp, garden produce and eggs (where gathered by way of tithe).

For Harrow to have an Archbishop, a Rector and a Vicar might, at first glance, seem an overly generous provision but it has to be remembered that the Archbishop himself, though Lord of the Manor, was only occasionally in residence. (Indeed, the exact location of the Manor House before the move to Headstone Manor in 1344 has still to be confirmed).

What is known, however, is that around 1200 the Archbishop created a subsidiary Rectory Manor whose Rectory Manor House almost certainly adjoined the church on the site of the house we now call The Grove. It was once known, significantly enough, as The Lord's Grove.

We know, too, that the Harrow rectors were themselves men of some eminence who held many such appointments; thus, they too would have been frequently absent from Harrow.

The newly appointed Vicar, however, was expected to be in personal residence and there is every reason to suppose that the very first Vicarage was in exactly the same position, hard by the church, as the present day building.

Even pluralists, of course, could come to love their churches and Elias of Dereham, Harrow's Rector at the time of the Endowment, is usually credited as the man responsible for the continued rebuilding of St Mary's.

In the past, there seems to have been a tendency to confuse Elias of Dereham with another of similar name who was himself a noted builder and King John's 'engineer' but contemporary opinion now identifies our Elias with the one-time steward to Archbishop Hubert Walter whose executor he became. Our Elias, however, seems to have been personally involved in work carried out at St Mary's. A Close Roll of 1242, for example, records an order from the King to the Archbishop's servants to supply Master Elias of Dereham with six baulks of timber for the making of a kiln (presumably to burn lime) for the chancel of the church.

In 1334 Archbishop Stratford acquired as his Middlesex residence the
still-existing Headstone Manor, here pictured between the World Wars.

He may also have been the man who pierced the west wall of the tower to permit a new
shafted window and to have added an internal staircase. In the process, his builders almost
certainly weakened the structure of the tower (which, in any event, had been built on sand
without proper foundations) requiring the provision of the first of the massive buttresses we
still see today.

Samuel Gardner also dates to this period the existing north and south doorways.

As far as the actual doors themselves are concerned, what we now regard as the north door
was, in fact, the original south door and principal entry to the church. This was removed for
its own protection during the mid-19th century restoration.

Today this door is remarkable for the size of its lock and case (measuring a yard in length,
a foot in width and four inches in thickness) and for the innumerable nails with which it is
studded, a reminder of the days when it served as a notice-board for every kind of parish
communication.

The opinion has occasionally been voiced that this second phase of rebuilding had to be
completed in time for a visitation by the then Archbishop, Boniface of Savoy, uncle of Henry
III's queen, Eleanor.

Boniface, one of the most unpopular men to hold the Primacy, certainly made a visitation
to Harrow in 1250. History, however, suggests that his visit was more of an undignified retreat
to comparative sanctuary following stormy scenes in London when, during an attempt to
exact monies from St Paul's and St Bartholomew's, Smithfield, it was discovered that the
Archbishop was wearing armour beneath his vestments.

ABOVE: A modern photograph taken in the Vicarage garden reveals the site's centuries-old proximity to Old Schools (right), the original building of Harrow School. BELOW: Widely accepted as the site of the original Rectory Manor, The Grove is now a Harrow School boarding house. (Photo: Sophie Powell)

LEFT: Stonework surrounding this 13th century lancet window in the chancel still carries traces of its original medieval painting. (Photo: Sophie Powell)
RIGHT: For centuries the massive nail-studded door on the north side of the Church provided the main entrance to St Mary's.

# ROYAL BREAK WITH ROME

On the accession of King Henry VIII in 1509, St Mary's was in the fullest sense a Catholic Church and thus little different in its ritual from every other church in Western Christendom. The Archbishops of Canterbury, too, were still the Lords of the Manor of Harrow as they had been since the year 825.

Yet at Henry's will — one is tempted to say whim — all this was to change dramatically. Even worse, the pendulum of change was to swing backwards and forwards throughout the three successive reigns of Henry's children — Edward, Mary and Elizabeth — and often at a truly lamentable cost to the life, liberty and conscience of their subjects.

It is sometimes overlooked that two, at least, of these reigns were relatively brief so it would be entirely possible for many of the parishioners of St Mary's to have lived through the whole sequence of events our history books somewhat loosely dub the Reformation. For example, a man of 20 when Henry died in 1547 would still have been but 61 when the defeat of the Spanish Armada in 1588 put paid to any real danger of armed foreign intervention in England's church affairs. But we must not jump ahead in a story whose tremendous impact locally as well as nationally warrants its telling at some length.

Obviously, whole books exist that detail the many and complex reasons why the great international Catholic Church of Western Europe finally broke up and gave rise to separate national churches no longer in allegiance to the Pope in Rome.

Fortunately for this narrative, the separation of the English Church was, in many ways, a simpler matter, occasioned not so much by differences of belief as by a quarrel between two strong-minded men — an English King and a Roman Pontiff.

The early years of Henry's reign, however, gave little clue to the turmoil ahead. His succession was both peaceful and popular for he had been acknowledged the heir apparent ever since the death of his brother, Arthur, in 1502. Moreover, his attack on the radical teachings of Martin Luther had quickly earned him both the gratitude of the Pope and the title 'Defender of the Faith' (which the English sovereign bears to this very day).

His personal life was not then unhappy although it is doubtful whether he ever bore for his wife — the Spanish Katharine of Aragon — the depth of love that, to the end of her days, she bore for him.

It was Henry's first marriage but Katharine had previously been married to his late brother (who was only 15 at the time) and it required a special Papal dispensation before the marriage could proceed.

When, some 18 years later, Katharine had failed to give him a male heir — all but a daughter, Mary, had been still-born or lived only a matter of weeks — Henry conveniently began to ask whether his marriage had offended against Scripture. More significantly, he queried whether the earlier Pope had exceeded his temporal authority in allowing the marriage to take place. (The fact that Henry had fallen in love with the beautiful Anne Boleyn only served to add ardour to his arguments).

So, knowing full well that nullity decrees were not beyond the reach of the rich and powerful, Henry ordered his Chancellor and erstwhile friend, Cardinal Wolsey, to arrange for the annulment of the marriage. But if Henry's thinking was correct, his timing was horribly wrong for the Pope, Clement VII, was in no position to offend the even more powerful Emperor Charles V — and Charles was Queen Katharine's nephew.

51

The Pope took refuge in procrastination and Wolsey was obliged to take the brunt of his sovereign's wrath, ultimately being indicted under the old statue of *praemunire* for having taken orders from a foreign power. Stripped of his Chancellorship, Wolsey only escaped the block by dying a merciful natural death.

With Wolsey gone — and his marriage to the tantalising Anne no closer — Henry decided, not for the first or last time, that bullying might succeed where diplomacy had failed. He promptly charged the whole English clergy with a breach of *praemunire*. Moreover, he insisted that the only way they could save themselves from punishment was to pay a hefty fine and to acknowledge him as Supreme Head of the English Church.

Having cowed the clergy, Henry used the anti-clericalism of many in Parliament to push through a series of bills all designed to cut the bonds with Rome. When Archbishop Warham died, Henry contrived (admittedly with the Pope's agreement) the consecration of his new-found friend and ally, Thomas Cranmer.

With the passing of the Act in Restraint of Appeals (which denied any appeal to the Holy See and asserted the King's position as Supreme Head of Church and State), the scene was set for a divorce from his Queen and the public announcement in April 1533 of his marriage to Anne Boleyn (which, in fact, had already taken place in secret).

The announcement came not a moment too soon for, in the September following, Anne gave birth to their first child. Ironically, it was not the longed-for boy — but a girl whom they christened Elizabeth.

This then, in fairly simplistic terms, was the start of the 'Reformation' in England though, as far as the ordinary churchgoer was concerned, there was, at first, very little in the way of change that could truly be termed 'reform'.

Instead, Henry turned his attention to the monasteries. Their dissolution was accomplished with the maximum gain to Henry's coffers and incalculable loss to the country's artistic heritage.

Much of this destruction, which was both vindictive and acquisitive, was shamefully carried out by the-then Rector of Harrow, Richard Layton.

It is often said that history recalls its villains more vividly than its saints and so it is with Layton, about whom we know a good deal more than many other early rectors.

Born of modest parentage in Cumberland around 1500, Layton nevertheless obtained a Cambridge education and, at only 22, was appointed to the sinecure Rectory of Stepney. It was around this time that he came to the attention of Thomas Cromwell, successor to Wolsey as Henry VIII's Chancellor. Cromwell pronounced his protegé 'dextrous and diligent' which seems to have meant that, whenever there was an especially dirty deed to be done, Layton could be relied upon to do it.

Layton positively fawned upon Cromwell. Inviting him to the Rectory House at Harrow, he wrote that 'Simeon was never so glad to see Christ, his master, as I shall be to see you'.

This particular letter also throws an interesting sidelight on the (perhaps surprising) size of the Harrow Rectory in the 1530s. 'If you had come to Harrow on Friday, your bed was ready', he wrote. 'You should have 20 beds in the town, where there has been no sickness this year, and a dozen in the parsonage'.

Layton also proved his worth to Cromwell by undertaking the leadership of the so-called Visitation of the Monasteries — in reality, a wholly cynical device designed to give Henry an accurate assessment of ecclesiastical revenues so that he could subsequently tap them to finance his own extravagant life-style. Layton was also instructed to provide — and, if necessary, manufacture — evidence that the monks and nuns were themselves consistently abusing their privileges.

# THE SUDBURY TRAITORS

Given the popular acceptance of Elizabeth as head of the English Church, it required singular courage, even recklessness, for any person to propound a contrary view. Yet the Sudbury Bellamy family remained unswerving in their dedication to the Roman Faith.

The Bellamys lived at Uxendon Manor (so-called though it was never a true manor), on the banks of the Brent some two or three miles from Harrow Hill. It was thus within the parish of St Mary's and, during the early years of Elizabeth's reign, the parish registers offer ample evidence that the heads of the household, William and Katherine Bellamy, paid at least lip service to the contemporary rules of the English Church.

The marriage of their eldest child and only daughter, Dorothy, to Anthony Frank or Frankyshe is recorded, as are the baptisms of six of their grandchildren. Yet, whatever they avowed in public, there can be little doubt that, in private, they continued to hold true to Roman ways and, by the late 1560s, word seems to have spread abroad that Uxendon Manor could be regarded — to use a modern term — as 'a safe house' for Catholic recusants.

Indeed, once the English recusant William Allen had founded a college overseas for the express purpose of training Catholic missionaries to England, many of its members ultimately found their way to Uxendon Manor. (By an interesting coincidence, the college was founded at Douay, that same French town that is currently twinned with Harrow).

By this time, the Papal Bull excommunicating Elizabeth and relieving her subjects of their allegiance had so unified the majority of her people that there was precious little sympathy around for those who chose to be recusants. For example, the reckless man who ventured to nail a copy of the Papal Bull on the door of the Bishop of London was promptly executed as a traitor.

Against this background, it was hardly surprising that Elizabeth's fourth Parliament in 1581 passed an act imposing a fine of 100 marks and a year's imprisonment on anyone hearing Mass. Yet, that very same year, the Bellamys were sheltering at Uxendon Manor one Father Richard Bristow, regarded as a key figure in the Catholic Mission to England. Though Uxendon Manor apparently had a secret chamber, it seems that Bristow lived there openly, passing himself off as 'Cousin Springe', a poor relation of Mrs Bellamy. More amazingly, when he died at Uxendon (and there is no reason to presume other than natural causes), the family so successfully continued the deception that Father Bristow was actually buried at St Mary's under his assumed name by the unsuspecting Protestant Vicar of Harrow, the Reverend Brian Crofts.

On that occasion, luck had run with the Bellamy family but the general climate of suspicion was soon to be heightened by an 'Act Against Jesuits, Seminary Priests and Other Such-like Disobedient Parsons'. This ordered all Roman Catholic priests to quit the kingdom within 40 days under penalty of high treason. It also made the offence of concealment punishable by 'imprisonment during the Queen's pleasure'.

Yet once William Bellamy, the head of the household, had died, the family seems to have thrown all caution to the winds and the Middlesex County Record of Indictments shows several counts against members of the family 'for not going to church, chapel or any other place of Common Prayer'.

Then, in 1586, they undertook the most desperate gamble of all, giving shelter to the man who was perhaps the most eagerly-sought fugitive of this troubled era. He was Anthony

Babington, the principal figure in what became known as the Babington Plot, a notorious conspiracy whose sole purpose was the assassination of Queen Elizabeth followed by the crowning of Mary, Queen of Scots.

The full details of an intensely complicated tale of plot and counter-plot may never be fully known; certainly, it is now widely accepted that the conspirators fell into a trap deliberately engineered by Sir Thomas Walsingham, Elizabeth's cunning Secretary of State and spy-catcher in chief.

Though Mary was being held virtually incommunicado in Fotheringay Castle in Northampton, Walsingham allowed a private postal service to be set up, whereby letters for the Scottish Queen were smuggled into the Castle in watertight containers inside the regular deliveries of beer. As he anticipated, treasonable evidence soon appeared in the form of a letter from Anthony Babington, who had idolised Mary for years, in which he spoke of six noble gentlemen who would be willing to kill Elizabeth on her behalf. An immediate hue and cry began for Babington and his fellow conspirators. At first, they seem to have hidden in the open country. Then, according to William Camden, the contemporary writer, 'being constrained by famine [they] went to an house of the Bellamys near Harrow Hill who were greatly addicted to the Romish religion. There they were hid in barns, fed and clothed in rusticated attire'.

Other contemporary reports suggest that a suspicious constable actually came to the door of the Manor but was persuaded to leave after Jerome Bellamy had stoutly denied any knowledge of the traitors, who were, in fact, hiding in a barn behind the house.

On Saturday, the eighth day of their flight, it is said that a priest came to Uxendon and, next day, not only heard Babington's confession but also took mass 'in a secret chapel'.

That same day, however, the house was surrounded and Babington, his four companions and two of the Bellamy sons were all taken prisoner. Inevitably, Babington and his confederates died hideous deaths which the Queen was reputed to have ordered 'be protracted to the extremity of pain'.

Jerome Bellamy, the second son, was tried as an accessory after the fact, convicted and also barbarously done to death at Tyburn. (The name, of course, survives locally in Harrow's Tyburn Lane which, then as now, is on the route to Marble Arch where the executions were carried out).

Other members of the Bellamy family also met cruel ends. Katherine Bellamy, who was by now aged and infirm, was committed to the Fleet Priosn and then to the Tower where, some time later, she died. Another of the Bellamy sons, Bartholomew, was apparently put to the rack so brutally that he died in prison even before he could be brought to trial.

Already imprisoned for his faith at the time of the Babington conspiracy, the fourth son, Robert Bellamy, was reported to have died by his own hand. This, of course, was highly unlikely in view of the beliefs that were responsible for his imprisonment; moreover, a suicide story was not uncommonly put about when prisoners had died on the rack.

Even the Bellamy family servants did not escape 'examination', one Richard Mascall confessing that he had been sent to guide the fugitives and bring them bread. In all, some half a dozen Harrow men and women, most in their twenties, were questioned. We know their names but, sadly, not their fates.

Though the Bellamy story seems to contradict the fact, torture was never part of the common law of England. It could, however, be administered with the Royal Assent and Elizabeth who, as Anne Boleyn's daughter, had herself constantly lived in the shadow of the rack and the block, had perforce to harden her heart. Nevertheless in the matter of the beheading of Mary, Queen of Scots — carried out at Fotheringay Castle in February 1587 — her true intent remains ambiguous.

When Parliament petitioned for the execution, Elizabeth's reply was couched in the following terms: 'If I say unto you that I mean not to grant your petition, by my faith I should say unto you more than perhaps I mean. And if I should say with you I mean to grant your petition, I should then tell you more than is fit for you to know. And thus I must deliver you an answer answerless'.

In the event, the turmoil did not cease with one Queen permitting the death of another for, within two years, Spain had launched its Armada in an attempt both to conquer England and to restore the power of the Papacy. It was, of course, an ignominious failure — a failure that not only enhanced Elizabeth's prestige but, more vitally, removed any real danger of foreign intervention in this country's religious affairs.

We can only guess what was actually happening within St Mary's throughout these dramatic events for, even after the Act of Uniformity, there was still considerable diversity of thought within the Church.

Brian Crofts, whom the Bellamys duped so convincingly, remained at Harrow virtually to the end of Elizabeth's 45 year reign. As we read earlier, St Mary's had already acquired a pulpit and Crofts would have been expected to preach regularly to his congregation. He would have used, too, the dignified English liturgy and the English Bible which, throughout the land, were helping this new English Church to grow in public esteem.

We can also assume Crofts' busy involvement in the work of St Mary's Vestry for, although the Vestry concept first emerged in the 14th century, it was the Elizabethan era that gave it the greatest powers and the toughest responsibilities. Thus, by the end of the century, the Vestry was the true administrative centre for the parish in both civil and church affairs.

Although adequate provision was made for the local aged, impoverished and sick, the problems of the wandering poor were harshly dealt with.

When the closing of the monasteries inevitably added to the numbers of poor roaming the countryside, Harrow's response was simply to command the constable to have sufficient stocks in which to punish them. Again, from a court roll of 1575, we learn that five vagrants at Harrow were sentenced to be flogged and burned on the ear.

Inevitably, life continued to be harsh for the religious non-conformer.

In 1592, Anne Bellamy, yet another member of the Uxendon Manor family, was held in the Gatehouse prison at Westminster 'as an obstinate recusant'. Here she seems to have fallen under the influence of the much-feared Richard Topcliffe, who allegedly got her with child and then married her off to Nicholas Jones, an underkeeper at the Gatehouse. It is often claimed that, under Topcliffe's influence, Anne yielded up further secrets of Uxendon Manor which led to the capture — and execution — of another noted priest, Father Robert Southwell. Topcliffe also seems to have tried his hand at blackmail, urging one Richard Bellamy to give Anne and Nicholas a house at Preston, though the elder Bellamy evidently refused.

An attempt has been made by 19th century historians such as Percy Thornton and Done Bushell to identify this house with John Lyon's Farm at Preston. They argue that John Lyon had died that year and that the Lyons and the Bellamys were known to have been not only neighbours but friends.

In the Lyon papers in the Harrow School muniments, there is, indeed, a record of a quittance to a loan earlier made by Bellamy to Lyon.

After the two signatures, Bellamy had appended in his own hand the name of two rebels of the time of Richard II — Jack Straw and Wat Tyler. It was almost certainly a joke. Yet it is tempting to wonder if there was perhaps just a hint of the rebel about John Lyon who, as we shall see, had every reason to profess gratitude to his Queen.

LEFT: The gravestone of John Lyon is now at the foot of the chancel steps. It once held the memorial brass mounted on a column in the nave. (Photo: Sophie Powell) RIGHT: Generations of Gerards are now remembered in the north transept, including William Gerard and his sister, Frances, commemorated by this fine alabaster memorial. (Photo: Sophie Powell)

# JOHN LYON'S SCHOOL

John Lyon remains one of the major figures in Harrow history yet, without wishing to diminish his achievements, he is best described as the re-founder of Harrow School rather than its actual founder.

As we have seen, there can be no doubt that a school of sorts already existed on Harrow Hill in his lifetime.

Lyon's great contribution was to take this School (which probably had suffered financially since the severance with the Archbishops) and to put it on an infinitely stronger footing, with a reasonable endowment, more professional management and a well-considered body of rules.

He seems to have set about this task much as any good businessman might do today, first enlisting the help of one of his more influential contacts — Sir Gilbert Gerard, who was Attorney General to the Queen. Sir Gilbert was also the brother of Lyon's neighbour, William Gerard of Flambards, the great local mansion named after a centuries-old Harrow family.

Lyon and Gerard may have also had the support of Dr John Caius, the refounder of the Cambridge College that bears his name, who lived in Ruislip and for whose College Lyon later endowed two scholarships.

With this degree of influential support, their cause seems to have found ready favour with Queen Elizabeth and, in the fourteenth year of her reign, she granted a Royal Charter for the establishment of their proposed foundation.

Nothing in the way of new building seems to have happened until 1615 when what we now know as Old Schools began to rise on its site adjoining St Mary's. By this time, both Lyon and his wife had died.

This delay in building, though obviously influenced by matters of finance, again suggests that there were adequate school premises already in existence.

While these were certainly located at some time in the Church House, it is just possible this School may have later moved into Flambards itself.

We can perhaps find a hint in the St Mary's burial registers where the entry for Anthony Rate (who died in 1611) describes him as 'Schoolmaster at Flambards, afterwards elected schoolmaster for the free schools'.

To allow a School at Flambards would have been entirely in character for Gerard, a notably public-spirited man who provided the town with a new pump house for the well at the top of West Street.

On the other hand, the entry may simply mean that Rate was at one time tutor to the Gerard household.

If this must remain a puzzle, we do know that Rate held the office of Head Master until his death, when he was succeeded by a Mr Bradley (though it would appear that neither of these gentlemen enjoyed the status or the salary of a proper head).

Further interest attaches to Rate's burial entry because of its use of the term 'free school', one of a number of contemporary indications that Lyon's benefaction was originally intended solely as a free school for local boys.

This was certainly the view taken by the parish and considerable hostility was voiced as the school became progressively more aristocratic. Nevertheless a more temperate attitude in the town might have acknowledged the obvious fact that such developments were largely of John Lyon's doing.

In his remarkably comprehensive Statutes for the running of the School, he clearly laid down that the Schoolmaster 'may receive over and above the youth of the inhabitants within this parish so many foreigners as the whole number may well be taught and, of these foreigners, he may take such stipend and wages as he can get'.

When the locals stayed away from the school because of its purely classical and, to them, largely useless curriculum, it was hardly surprising that the Master should welcome outsiders from whom he could collect a handsome fee. It was largely inevitable, too, that these boys should come from a different social background which, in itself, was to be a source of further tension between 'town' and 'gown'.

Happily, John Lyon left no such loopholes in the matter of religious instruction (although, as we shall see, the manner and place of that instruction was to change over the years).

Every scholar, his Statutes decreed, was to be taught the Lord's Prayer, the Articles of the Faith, the Ten Commandments 'and other of the chief parts of the Catechism and principal points of Christian religion in English first and after in Latin'.

The role of worship in the school day was also clearly defined. 'The first thing to be done in the morning after they be assembled and the last in the evening before their departure', proclaimed the Statutes, 'shall be upon their knees with reverence to say prayers to be conceived by the Master'.

John Lyon was equally insistent in the matter of church attendance, laying down that 'All the Scholars shall come to the church and there hear divine service and the Scripture read or interpreted with attention and reverence'.

He even made financial provision to allow the Governors 'to provide and procure 30 good, learned and Godly sermons to be preached yearly for ever in the parish church'.

As the early headmasters were themselves in holy orders, they seemed to have shared this duty with the local Vicar but, once secular headmasters became the norm, the Vicar wholly assumed the task. Over the years the original payment (six shillings and eightpence per sermon) grew into something approaching a salary — £15 in 1622, £25 in 1763.

Today, however it seems that only the enthusiastic historian has heard of the John Lyon Sermons and it is difficult to discover precisely when the practice ceased.

Interestingly enough, we know the identity of the first boy to benefit from John Lyon's benefaction. He was Macharie Wildblud and, appropriately enough, he was the son of that Humphrey Wildblud who was Vicar of Harrow at the close of Elizabeth's reign.

Whether or not John and Joan Lyon also had a son remains something of a mystery.

Sir Gilbert Gerard is on record as saying of Lyon 'He hath no children'; nor are there any appropriate records in the parish registers. Yet, from an early lithograph made of the Lyon brass in St Mary's, we can see that the two adult figures were once accompanied by a third tiny figure of unidentified sex standing (some say, kneeling) between them.

The assumption is that this figure was a child who died in infancy and that this part of the brass was carelessly damaged when the whole memorial was transferred from the floor of the church to its present wall-mounting in the nave. (Certainly both the adult figures lost their feet in the process).

Had this child been a boy who outlived his parents, John Lyon's act of beneficence might have been very different — and Harrow itself a very different place.

Today, it is not only John and Joan Lyon who are remembered at St Mary's. The death of William Gerard in 1584 is recorded on a wall plaque alongside a splendid alabaster monument to a later William Gerard, shown at prayer with his sister Frances. (They were both married but it seems that their partners preferred to be remembered in churches elsewhere).

As long ago as May 1896 the local historian Ethert Brand complained that the monument languished in 'an ill-chosen spot for such a fine specimen of late Tudor work'. Today, almost one hundred years later, it still remains in a somewhat gloomy corner of the north transept.

Removed from the original tomb, possibly for its protection, the John
Lyon brass was badly damaged in the process. (Photo: Sophie Powell)

The ruins of Stanmore Old Church consecrated in 1632, as they looked in 1906; they still stand in the grounds of the present St John's.

# A COMMUNITY DIVIDED

The 20th century has witnessed enough examples of the hideousness of civil conflict to make us realise the full horror of the War which in 1642 set Englishman against Englishman.

Though religion, politics and social problems were all inextricably woven into its causes, at the heart of the War lay the fact that some 20 years after the death of a Queen who could do little wrong, England had both a King (Charles I) who could do little right and an Archbishop (Laud) who too closely allied the Church with the cause of the monarch.

The perhaps inevitable result was that the Puritans, those Protestant clergy and laity who desired a more simple service and ritual, became ever more closely allied to the growing Parliamentary opposition to the King.

Just where Harrow's Vicar, Thomas Launce, stood in this controversy is hard to assess although we know that his predecessor, Humphrey Wildblud, had been dismissed from an earlier living for his Puritan leanings (although this was long before Puritanism had become a force in the land).

Launce may well have been a very different kind of man from Wildblud, having been the first proper Head Master of John Lyon's School from 1615 to 1621 when he frequently helped Wildblud in the preaching of the sermons John Lyon had ordained in his will. His brother, the Reverend William Launce was, in fact, still the Usher of the School during his incumbency.

Similarly, we can only guess at the local political climate although local historian, Walter Druett, found evidence that Harrow offered some of the strongest resistance when, in 1635, King Charles attempted to increase revenue by imposing the so-called Ship Money on inland as well as coastal counties. Druett claims that, in Harrow alone, the King's Collectors took 40 distresses (that is, the holding of property against debts).

Indeed, far from being the Royalist stronghold one might expect from the presence of the now 30 year old School and a number of distinguished residents, Harrow was not lacking in active Parliamentarians.

In particular, the great house Flambards was then occupied by another Gilbert Gerard, a descendant of Elizabeth's Attorney General, who was both a Member of Parliament for Middlesex (sitting in five Parliaments between 1623-40) and the husband of Mary Barrington, first cousin to Oliver Cromwell.

According to the Calendar of Staff Papers, Domestic, Gerard actually raised a regiment on Cromwell's behalf which, perforce, must have included many Harrow men.

Both Sir Francis Rewse of Headstone and Sir Richard Page of Uxendon were of the King's party, exemplifying the cruel divisions which rent even the smallest community.

The nearest actual fighting to Harrow was almost certainly at Brentford but a dispatch of 1643, discovered last century by Ethert Brand, suggests that there may have been a military establishment on the Hill for it lists Harrow among the places to which officers had been sent to receive their orders.

Traditionally, however, the Hill has chosen to associate itself with the King. Today the site of one of the old town wells (outside the Harrow School Art Schools) bears a plaque claiming that Charles watered his horses at this well before his flight and eventual defeat.

It is an attractive conceit but the plaque would carry greater authenticity if we did not know that it was erected as recently as 1925 nearly three centuries after the event it supposedly commemorates. The well itself was filled in when the Harrow School house, Rendalls, was built in 1854.

The mantle of Royal supremacy having fallen from the King, it was promptly picked up by the House of Commons which made itself the supreme judge in ecclesiastical matters.

Soon, all parishioners over 18 were obliged to accept the Solemn League and Covenant, taking an oath that they would bring the Church 'to the nearest conjunction and uniformity in religion'.

At much the same time, the so-called Westminster Assembly, consisting of a mix of English Puritan divines, Scottish Presbyterian ministers and zealous laymen, set about reforming the Church by drawing up a new book of public worship and a new system of church government. They worked quickly and on 4 January 1645 (the same day that Archbishop Laud went to his execution), the Commons abolished the Book of Common Prayer in favour of the so-called Directory.

This, the only legal service book as it was called, made it an offence to kneel for Communion or to use any kind of symbolism in a sacred context, even a ring in marriage.

Although we can assume that Vicar Launce had already taken the Covenant, these latest moves may have been more than his conscience would permit for, in 1645, he was ejected from St Mary's and replaced by the Reverend Thomas Pakeman.

Whatever the contemporary feeling in the parish, hindsight suggests that Harrow should have felt fortunate that the new Vicar was an educated man and properly ordained. Many vacant benefices at this time were filled with Presbyterians or independent ministers who had either been ordained by the Presbyterians or had received no form of ordination. Other pulpits were simply seized by ambitious men without any kind of authority.

*The Survey of Church Livings In Middlesex At The Time Of The Commonwealth* lists Pakeman as 'a constant preaching minister (presented by George Pitt  Esq) who supplies and performs the said cure and hath for his salary the profits of the said vicarage which are not now (offerings and such-like duties ceasing) worth above 50 pounds an annum if the tithes of Pinner were duly paid; also 50 a year more granted by the Honourable Committee of Plundered Ministers for the increase of his maintenance.'

The reference to Pinner is an interesting one in that it suggests that the good people of Pinner had withheld their tithes at least until the Government had responded to a petition of 1641, praying that 'they have liberty to make choice of a lecturer whom they will maintain at their own choice'.

Essentially it was a 'lecturer' rather than a preacher they were seeking for, as Walter Druett points out, the Puritans were quick to realise 'the common people were most easily stirred and animated by the demagogue'.

The subsequent appointment of a Mr William Rowles appears to have been acceptable but the argument that Pinner chapel should be made a parish church 'intier of itself' continued to gather force for at least another century.

A 19th century book *Nonconformity in Herts* also mentions Pakeman (who was, at one time, also minister of Hadham, Herts) stating that 'at Harrow he was in great esteem with Sir Gilbert Gerard and soon had the instruction and boarding of several children of persons of quality, and preached as he had opportunity'.

More important, it seems likely that Pakeman's relationship with the highly influential Gerard helped to spare St Mary's from the worst kind of iconoclastic vindictiveness. Nevertheless, at some time, by some hand, the figures of the apostles on the nave roof were undoubtedly defaced.

That Parliamentary troops could be as cruel and predatory in Harrow as elsewhere was discovered by Ethert Brand when researching his local history series for the parish magazine. Among Historical Manuscripts then held at the House of Lords, he found a parchment in which Margery Page, a widow, petitioned the Lords 'in her great extremity and that her deeds, goods and clothes may be restored to her'.

Buried in the churchyard in 1794, the notorious miser Daniel Dancer left
a fortune, including £2,500 buried in a dung heap.

When Saunders showed no signs of changing his ways — indeed he buried several more
strangers between April and July — the Vestry referred the whole issue to the Court of
Arches, then as now the principal court of the Archbishop of Canterbury. (The unusual name
was derived from its original meeting place in the Church of St Mary LeBow, otherwise Santa
Maria de Arcubus).

It took some three years for the parish to receive the verdict of the Dean of Arches — in
effect, the judge — but at least it was the one they had sought.

Saunders was to be admonished for his conduct; moreover, he was to be informed that the
churchwardens did not give leave 'for the taking down of any of the pews in the church, nor
for breaking up the pavement for making any grave there, until the fees due to the parish is
paid, and they are satisfied that the pews shall be set up again and the pavement amended
without putting the parish to any charge'.

Saunders seems to have lived down the incident for he remained at St Mary's for a full fifty
years which saw, at least, one other incident of quite literally high drama.

On a Spring morning in 1763 during what one contemporary newspaper described as 'the
greatest storm of rain and hail . . . ever remembered by the oldest person', St Mary's spire was
struck by lightning. Burning furiously, the weather cock and some 15 feet fell away 'on that
side facing Sir John Rushout's', (now The Grove).

Fortunately, the boys of Harrow School were so prompt in giving the alarm there was no
time for the timber roof to catch fire and 'three-score' men were said to have stripped away
the smouldering lead.

Over one hundred years later, one of their number, William Timberlake, was still being
hailed as a hero in the official *Handbook to Harrow Hill*. The 1850 edition tells us that 'the hat
and coat he wore at the time were preserved for many years by his family who still reside in
Harrow'. Apparently the items still 'bore singular evidence of his activity and danger, being
nearly covered with molten lead which had fallen from the spire'.

In 1994, one looks in vain for the whereabouts of 'this curious memorial' although,
interestingly enough, there are still eleven Timberlakes in the local telephone directory.

ABOVE: Originally the Perpetual Curate for Pinner, Walter Williams became Vicar of Harrow in 1776. His wife was descended from Charles II and Nell Gwynn. BELOW: Undated view of old Pinner where Walter Williams chose to live and whose church he chose for his burial.

82

# A ROYAL BRIDE

There cannot be many parishes whose vicar brings home a bride of Royal descent or whose personal fortune allows him to abandon his vicarage for a grand home elsewhere. But St Mary's had just such a man in Walter Williams, who first came to the district as Assistant Curate at Pinner in 1764.

After ten years, during which the Pinner chapelry was finally severed from St Mary's, Williams was himself made Vicar of Harrow and, since he saw no reason to resign his Pinner appointment, the two positions were vested in the one man.

As a later vicar wryly comments in Druett's *Pinner Through The Ages*, 'it is interesting to imagine Williams standing every quarter day in Pinner porch and taking money from one pocket as Vicar of Harrow and transferring it to the other pocket as Perpetual Curate of Pinner'.

In any event, a degree of opportunism seems not entirely foreign to his character. In 1779 he added to his incomes the Rectorship of Throwley in Kent and, thus armed, paid court to a highly important local resident, Mary Beauclerc.

Mary was not young — in fact nearer 40 than 30 — but she happened to be the grand-daughter of no less a personage than Charles Beauclerc, the elder of the two sons born to Charles II by the actress Nell Gwynn.

According to the invaluable researches of the Pinner historian, Patricia A. Clarke, it seems the family were still in royal favour for Martha, the mother, had been maid-of-honour to George II's Queen, Caroline. A brother, too, had married into the Drummonds, the wealthy banking family of Great Stanmore.

In 1781, at St George's, Hanover Square, Walter Williams duly married his heiress and, some seven years later, they purchased one of Pinner's most impressive houses, the present Pinner House, for an equally impressive £700.

As they required neither the Vicarage nor the curate's Pinner accommodation, Williams saw the wisdom of letting the former to the fast-growing Harrow School and, to this end, he set about having it rebuilt.

To this day, visitors to the Vicarage drawing room can see an inscription carved in the wall that reads 'W. Williams built this house'.

Though it obviously paid him to attend to the fabric of the Vicarage, Williams seems to have been among the many Georgian clergymen who allowed their churches to fall into some disrepair although, in mitigation, he himself seems to have been the victim of yet another dispute over the cost of repairs.

This time, however, it appears that the ruinous state of the chancel was of far more than local concern.

There was even correspondence about it in the pages of the nationally-read *Gentleman's Magazine* whose September 1786 edition carried an indignant letter from a visitor to St Mary's who claimed that there was 'not a whole pane of glass left in the windows, very large cracks in the walls and the east window obliged to be propped up to prevent its falling'.

The reason for the dilapidation seems to have been equally well known to this correspondent, a local inhabitant having informed him of a 'a dispute between the Lord of the Manor and the proprietors of the great tithes'. This last piece of information seems to have particularly outraged the writer, prompting him to remark that 'in whichever of these gentlemen the fault lies, I am convinced that neither of them has a stable for their cattle in such a bad condition as the place for the Lord's Table is at Harrow'.

Nor was the correspondent alone in his condemnation for a further letter in the November issue also referred to 'the shameful condition' of Harrow Church and expressed the hope that the Bishop of the Diocese would interfere.

In fact, we know that the churchwardens of the day, William Seger and Thomas Hill, had already lodged a formal complaint and, in an extract from the Registers of the Deanery of Croydon dated February 1788, we can still read the answers made by Mary Herne, Spinster, then the lessee of the Dean and Chapter of Christ Church, Oxford.

Her comments seem all too familiar to anyone aware of the long-running controversy of the previous century; in fact, Miss Herne actually restated the terms of the earlier arbitration, claiming that, since that date, the chancel had never been repaired at the sole expense of the owner or the lessees of the great tithes.

Although no precise details have been found, we can safely assume that some repairs were carried out at this time, albeit of a patchwork kind; certainly in 1795, Daniel Lyson's guide book *The Environs of London* could devote considerable space to St Mary's without any mention of dilapidation.

In just about every way, it seems likely that Walter Williams lived some remove from the majority of his parishioners though, for the first few years, relationships seem to have been harmonious enough. He was undoubtedly fond of bells for the first peal ever rung at St Mary's took place during his incumbency; in fact, a peal board commemorating the event on 7 May 1780 still hangs in the belfry.

Times, however, were greatly changing and, all over the known world, ordinary men and women were challenging the status quo with results as dramatic and far-reaching as the War of American Independence and the downfall of the monarchy in France.

Even the boys of Harrow School staged their own revolt in 1805 when the young Byron was among those involved in a well organised campaign against the appointment as Head Master of Dr George Butler. (The boys favoured the promotion of second master, Mark Drury). According to Thornton's history, written almost within living memory of the event, Harrow pupils succeeded in blockading the road to London so that 'for several days the paralysis of authority was complete'.

In the early years of the century, there was also considerable local acrimony about the enclosure of waste and common-field land, for in 1802 the chief proprietors had agreed to support a Bill for inclosure which, whatever its intentions, had the ultimate effect of giving additional land to the biggest landowners.

It was against this background that some of the good parishioners of St Mary's now began to express their anger at what they saw as an abuse of John Lyon's intentions for Harrow School. By the early 1800s, the little local school had become what Thornton described with every justification as 'the most patrician school assemblage of which record remains'.

Claiming that their own boys were being squeezed out by well-to-do foreigners, the Parish sent a memorial to the Bishop of London who replied, somewhat cagily, that it was not proper for him to interfere in a matter of such moment without judicial directions.

R. B. Fisher, who signed himself 'Chairman of the Committee, appointed by Unanimous Vote of the Vestry to inquire into the Abuses of Harrow School', sent what was — for its time — a strongly worded riposte. 'My Lord, we desire no change, we ask no boon', he wrote 'but in all humility are seeking, as becomes us, to support, preserve and maintain the best birthright and inheritance of the parishioners of Harrow, the free education of our children and proper distribution of the charities so kindly intended and yet so shamefully withheld from us'.

There the matter seems to have rested for a couple of decades when, as we shall read later, the Parish took the School to law — and lost!

Around the year 1800 and with much the same challenging spirit, the officials of the church perpetrated what today seems an astonishing act of vandalism.

They threw out the simple and beautiful Purbeck marble font which, by then, had already been in use for some 600 years. They replaced it with what one contemporary described as 'a wash-hand basin-looking thing' though it was probably of 18th century plated metal. It carried the names of the current churchwardens, Charles Marlham and John M. Bliss, together with an inscription reading 'The Laver of Regeneration' and a set of initials supposedly those of Dr Samuel Garth, the well-known author of *The Dispensary*. Since Garth died in 1718 and is, in fact, buried at St Mary's, the font was presumably not a new one and one cannot but wonder where it had been before.

This interloping font might still be in place today but for an article in the January 1827 issue of Hone's *Every Day & Table Book* which described how 'the feelings of one parishioner — to the honour of her sex, a female — were outraged by this act of parochial vandalism'. The lady, who seems to have been the Mrs Leith then running the Dame's House at the Vicarage, sensibly preserved the font from destruction by placing it in a walled nook in her garden. Here it remained for some 40 years until William Winckley, then the Vestry Clerk of the parish, happened to borrow a copy of the very same *Table Book* from the Head Master's Library. Horrified to discover the details of the original font's removal, he stirred up such an agitation locally that it was ultimately restored to the church.

For a while, the usurping font seems to have been used as a plant container in the garden of Hogarth Cottage in Crown Street and the Rev Hugh Blackburne, Vicar of St Mary's in the early 1960s, claimed that it had been loaned, first to St Andrew's, Sudbury and later, to St Peter's, West Harrow, before either of these churches had permanent fonts of their own. Nevertheless its present whereabouts appear to be unknown.

We can only assume that Vicar Williams was a consenting party to the whole sorry affair though, by March 1807, he was also at odds with his parishioners.

In the event, all it took was a touch of high-handedness whereby Williams reported to the Vestry that 'by custom' he would nominate one of the churchwardens for the ensuing year.

Since the members of the Vestry were obviously satisfied with the services of Mr John Foster and Mr John Higgs, they not only made their own nomination but promptly adjourned to the Crown and Anchor for a further meeting.

Here, the real cause of their anger was revealed. It seemed that Mr Williams, like Mr Saunders before him, had been burying strangers both in the church and the churchyard; furthermore, 'all fees received by the Vicar were not due to the Vicar but to the Parish'.

Doubtless at the prompting of older parishioners who would at least have heard about the events of the previous century, the meeting agreed to inform the Archbishop of Canterbury that the Vicar's behaviour was 'contrary to the express direction of a Decree pronounced in the Court of Arches'.

Just what happened next is not entirely clear but it seems likely that the Court had been made aware of Williams' increasing age and infirmity (he was by then 71). Lord Northwick must also have realised that a new appointment could not be long delayed for the previous year he had conveyed the advowson of the living to a certain Robert Markham for the sum of £3,500.

As it happened, Williams lived on, and a change in Markham's circumstances prompted him to give Lord Northwick the opportunity to buy it back again (though it cost him £1,500 above the price he had received).

St Mary's Font was used as a garden ornament — from an early 19th century magazine article calling attention to this scandal.

Meanwhile, the quarrel over the churchwardens continued with increasing bitterness for, when the day for the appointment of the wardens came round again, we are told Mr Williams handled the matter 'in a hasty and clandestine manner before many of the inhabitants . . . had time to assemble'.

This so angered the always outspoken R. B. Fisher that he lodged an official protest in which he declared 'the conduct of the Vicar in this instant must be considered as a gross insult upon the parish'.

Matters so far deteriorated that as late as May 1810, four of the most influential men in the community — Lord Northwick, George Butler, then Head Master of Harrow, and his two most senior masters, Mark Drury and Harry Drury, felt obliged to present a further protest.

The controversy, they declared, was 'tending to destroy the tranquility of the parish and to create dissension between our fellow parishioners which we most seriously deplore'.

Yet, despite their intervention, the controversy dragged on until the April of 1811 when the election of candidates was put — not before time — to an open vote and a Mr George Clark, proposed by the curate, the Rev Samuel Evans, and Lord Northwick, and a Mr William Eastwick were elected by a majority of 69 to 55. By then, however, the Reverend Walter Williams had died.

At this juncture, it is hard to say whether parish priest and parish were ever truly reconciled for most of the Vicar's duties were then being performed by the Reverend Evans.

Whether his decision was dictated by convenience or spite, it is a fact that Williams chose not to be buried at St Mary's but closer to home at Pinner, where he was subsequently joined by his wife and their one daughter.

When alterations were being made to Pinner Church in 1956, it was reported that their coffins were still clearly visible in the vaults beneath the chancel.

ABOVE: First of Harrow School's buildings, shown around 1795 when local boys had already given way to sons of the aristocracy. BELOW: Only some 25 years separate this Harrow School picture from that dated 1795, but rapid school growth has meant the addition of a new wing.

This Victorian view of the churchyard was obviously inspired by Byron's
widely publicised practice of scribbling atop the Peachey Stone.

# CUNNINGHAM, BYRON & THE TROLLOPES

John Cunningham lived so long, achieved so much, was seen as either friend or adversary by so many (often very famous) people, that it seems amazing that he still awaits a full-scale biography. In the meantime, it is good that we have sympathetic studies of the man and his era by history students such as Audrey Boardman and Agnes L. Wyatt to whom this writer is much indebted.

For all that Cunningham's Harrow career encompassed the first exciting quarter century of Victoria's reign, he himself was born in 1780, half-way through the reign of George III. He also seems to have been born into what a later, more socially-conscious, generation would have termed 'trade', albeit trade of some style and substance — almost certainly, Cunningham and Evans, the hatters and hoziers of 163 Piccadilly.

His detractors were rarely to allow him to forget this comparatively lowly beginning, not least because Cunningham in his maturity had the manner and appearance of — as Thomas Trollope, the novelist's brother, put it — 'a more gentlemanly man than any of the Harrow masters of that day'.

In formative influence, however, his father's hats were as nothing compared with his mother's church-going and, from an early age, John Cunningham was taken to hear the great Evangelical preachers of the day. It was, therefore, especially appropriate that it was to Cambridge, then one of the two great centres for Evangelicalism (the other was Clapham), that he went as an undergraduate.

In 1802, the young Cunningham was ordained as curate of Ripley in Surrey, later moving to nearby Ockham where, some seven years later, he received a — not wholly unexpected — call from the Reverend John Venn, the noted Evangelical Rector of Clapham.

Venn was in need of a curate and Cunningham proved to be the ideal choice. By then, too, Cunningham had already made the first of two marriages that were both personally happy and socially advantageous.

His bride was Sophia Williams, daughter of Robert Williams, a Dorset banker who had moved to the mansion of Moor Park to be nearer his London business, later known as Williams Deacons Bank. John and Sophia, who were married at Rickmansworth parish church in 1805, became close friends with John Venn and moved readily and easily into the so-called 'Clapham Sect', the name given to the notably distinguished congregation to whom Venn ministered at Holy Trinity Church. Their number included the great abolitionist, William Wilberforce, and Henry Thornton, a City banker in whose home at Battersea Rise the 'Sect' regularly met and where the successful campaign against slavery was largely planned.

The Claphamites also showed their practical Christianity in the foundation of the Church Missionary Society and the British and Foreign Bible Society, both of which were to make considerable calls upon Cunningham's time and talents.

The Cunninghams were undoubtedly as happy with Venn as he was with them, 'What friends I have lost', Venn later wrote when, in 1811, Cunningham's father-in-law apparently purchased for him the living of St Mary's (the advowson having recently been bought back by Lord Northwick).

Cunningham's surviving letters are somewhat ambiguous on the circumstances of his appointment and he was popularly supposed to have spread the word that he owed the Harrow living to his having preached before Lord Northwick.

As Lord Northwick was not known for his church-going let alone his appreciation of its finer points, this was received in some quarters with a degree of mirth, Thomas Trollope later writing that the story was one that 'no inhabitant, clerk or layman, would have believed in the case of his Lordship if the preacher had been St Paul'.

Whatever the truth of the matter, Cunningham was not backward in asking his Lordship for further favours. While admitting that it would ill become him 'to grasp at more', an early letter to his patron continued 'still as I have a brother soon to enter the Church whose society at Pinner would be a great delight to me, I cannot but rejoice in the smallest hope of placing him there'. His hopes proved well justified and, for several years, the Reverend Francis Cunningham, five years his junior, served as his Curate.

If the skies over Clapham had been consistently blue, at Harrow they soon began to darken with clouds that not infrequently erupted into storm.

For a start, there were many High Anglicans in Harrow to whom Cunningham's Evangelical background and beliefs were anathema. Nor was he the kind of man to bend his opinions to the prevailing climate; 'indeed, Lord Teignmouth wrote to Samuel Wilberforce in 1812, 'his zeal was apt to exceed the precise measure of discretion'.

For example, within a couple of years of his arrival, Cunningham burst into print with a book *The Velvet Cushion* which was to run into ten editions. Purporting to be the 'autobiography' of a pulpit cushion, it was in fact an Evangelical's unblinking look at the changes that had taken place in religious practice in England since the time of Mary Tudor. This was followed by *A World of Souls*, again a religious treatise, but presented — less successfully — in the guise of a novel. 'We cannot say such phoney disguises altogether please our taste', wrote one reviewer.

In 1820, when King George IV sought to be rid of Queen Caroline through accusations of misconduct, Cunningham publicly crossed swords with the MP, Samuel Whitbread, over the latter's organisation of a public meeting to arouse feminine support for the Queen. Cunningham insisted that the time had come to stay 'the plague of political anarchy and moral pollution', and this decidedly unpopular view prompted so many threatening letters that 'I think it absolutely necessary to keep, at least for a short time, out of the public assemblies', he wrote to a friend 'and to stay at home and cheer my wife'.

Absences from the parish seem to have been routine in the early years of his ministry for he travelled tirelessly on behalf of the C.M.S. and the British and Foreign Bible Society. (The former made him a Life Governor as early as 1818).

Throughout all these activities, the Harrow School authorities (with the exception of the Drury faction, of whom we shall hear more) seem to have exercised considerable forbearance.

Possibly the School hoped that Cunningham's Evangelicalism — with its emphasis on moral probity — would serve as a recommendation to prospective parents perhaps fearful of the School's (well deserved) reputation for rowdyism in the town. It is certainly a fact that, after Cunningham became a School governor in 1819, the School roll began to rise once more.

It seems likely, too, that he had the friendship and support of the Harrow schoolmaster, Samuel Ellis Batten, who held the School house, The Grove, since Batten had married one of John Venn's daughters.

In 1822, however, Cunningham became a central figure in a genuine *cause célèbre* whose reverberations were felt well beyond Harrow.

The innocent cause was a five-year-old child who had recently died from influenza in   a far-off Italian convent. Her name was Allegra and she was the illegitimate daughter (by Clare Clairmont) of Lord Byron, one of the most celebrated (some would say notorious) men in the realm.

Having been notably happy as a schoolboy at Harrow, Byron felt it appropriate that Allegra should be brought home and buried at St Mary's. In a letter to his publisher, John Murray, he identifies the Peachy Stone in the churchyard as his favourite spot but adds 'as I wish to erect a tablet to her memory it will be better to have the body deposited in the church'. He also expressed the wish that the funeral 'be as private as is consistent with decency; and I hope that Henry Drury [his former tutor] will read the service over her'.

There were many locally, however, who felt that, given the child's illegitimacy, common decency would not permit either a church burial or a commemorative tablet. Cunningham himself was totally opposed to the idea of a tablet, writing to John Murray that 'whatever he [Byron] may wish in the moment of his distress . . . he will afterwards regret that he should have taken pains to proclaim to the world what he will not, I am sure, consider as honourable to his name'.

The little known fact that Cunningham had by then become friendly with Annabella Milbanke, Byron's wife and mother of his only true daughter, Ada, may well have influenced his decision. Even Byron seems to have been taken aback by his wife's appearance on the Harrow scene.

Later, he was to write 'they say that she [Allegra] was to be buried and epitaphed opposite Lady B's pew . . . God help me! I didn't know that Lady B. had ever been in Harrow Church and should have thought it the very last place she would have chosen'.

In fact, 'Lady B' had become friendly with John Cunningham's brother, Francis, who was by now the parson at Pakefield, near Lowestoft on the Suffolk coast. Francis Cunningham had then organised a meeting with John after which Byron's wife had written (somewhat ambiguously): 'I have talked to Cunningham a good deal about Lord Byron which his Harrow connection with him naturally led to and found him very accessible to the Truth'.

Unsurprisingly, John Cunningham's opposition in the matter of Allegra's burial was echoed by his Churchwarden, James Winkley who, on behalf of the parish, formally lodged an objection. At a subsequent Vestry Meeting, attended 'by all the masters . . . and sundry of the leading parishioners', it was agreed that the child might be buried but that no commemorative stone should be raised.

This decision seems to have been upheld by successive Vicars of Harrow right up to the 1980s although, at the Byron Centenary Service in 1924, the Reverend Edgar Stogdon commented that 'it seemed a little inconsistent that the generation that pardoned Nelson so unquestionably (his illegitimate daughter actually lived and died in Pinner) could be so mercilessly unforgiving to Byron'.

Finally, in 1980, renewed efforts on the part of the Byron Society were responsible for a stone being erected, immediately outside the church to the right of the south porch. (Even so, being at ground level, it is all too easy to overlook).

In the 170 or so years since Allegra's death (years in which the church has undergone extensive restoration), the exact location of Allegra's grave seems to have been lost; indeed, the only substantial reference the writer has ever seen comes in a letter dated 1899.

The writer was the-then incumbent, the Reverend F. Hayward Joyce, who claimed 'the grave is under the first pew on the right hand side as you enter the S. door'.

Although Cunningham's actions throughout the Allegra affair were undoubtedly supported by the parish as a whole, they further soured his unhappy relationship with members of the Drury family, and through them, with the Trollopes.

Since our contemporary view of Cunningham can easily be coloured by the decidedly hostile outbursts of these two highly vocal families, some further explanation might be helpful.

Fanny Trollope, in particular, seems to have taken a violent dislike to John Cunningham almost from the moment of her arrival in Harrow.

Her husband Thomas, having pursued a none-too-successful career as a London barrister, now fancied himself as a Middlesex farmer and, to this end, rented from Lord Northwick some 157 acres in the area of the present Julian Hill. Here, in the expectation of a large inheritance (never, in fact, to be realised), he promptly built himself a sizeable residence which, though much altered, still stands today.

By the time the future novelist Anthony Trollope was ready for Harrow School, there had been such a sharp decline in the family's fortunes that they were obliged to find a tenant for their grand house.

The fact that the new tenant proved to be John Cunningham can hardly have endeared him to the proud and headstrong Fanny. (Anthony, too — as his autobiography testifies — neither forgot nor forgave the fact that, for a while, he was obliged to live in a tumble-down farmhouse at Harrow Weald before the family were able to return to the farm house that stood on the Julian Hill estate).

It is often said that Fanny Trollope exacted a cruel revenge by basing the central character of her novel *The Vicar of Wrexhill* on Cunningham. Many contemporaries professed to recognise the connection and Samuel Wilberforce, son of the great abolitionist, even wrote to a friend that 'The Vicar of Wrexhill is meant, you know, for the Vicar of Harrow. It is a most abominable personal attack!'.

In later years, too, *What I Remember*, the autobiography of Anthony Trollope's brother, Thomas, seized every opportunity to belittle Cunningham.

To quote only one example, he described how an exceedingly pretty girl of some 18 years or so had come to his mother with a long defence of the Vicar.

'My Mother, suddenly looking her straight in the eyes, said "Did he kiss you, Carrie?", "Yes, Mrs. Trollope. He did give me the kiss of peace. I am sure there was no harm in that!" "None at all, Carrie. For I am sure you meant none", returned my mother . . . "but, remember, Carrie, that the kiss of peace is apt to change its quality if repeated".'

Though harmless enough in itself, the story carries a much sharper sting if one realises that in *The Vicar of Wrexhill*, the eponymous cleric is overly fond of his young parishioners.

Trollope also wrote disparagingly of Cunningham's involvement in the Allegra affair — 'the storm that was raised in the tea-cup of the Harrow world' — accusing him of 'innate and invincible flunkyism' in his dealings with Lord Byron.

Fanny Trollope was even inspired to write a lengthy satirical poem about the affair which so delighted Henry Drury that he presented her with a quarto page on which Byron himself had copied out one of his poems, including a stanza suppressed at publication. This became a proud possession which, together with her poem, Fanny Trollope was in the habit of displaying to any visitors who showed the slightest interest in the matter.

As a footnote to the story, it is worth recording that, even in rural Suffolk, Francis Cunningham seems to have enjoyed as interesting a life as his brother. Not only did he marry a sister of the Quaker prison reformer, Elizabeth Fry, he befriended George Borrow, the idiosyncratic writer of *Lavengro* and *The Romany Rye*.

Following an introduction from the Cunninghams, Borrow actually walked from Norwich to London for an interview with the Secretaries of the British and Foreign Bible Society. He obviously impressed them for they later sent him to St Petersburg to oversee the publication of a New Testament translated into Manchu-Tartar!

Both Cunningham brothers remained friendly with Byron's wife (and, from 1824, his widow). John Cunningham even entertained her at Harrow.

It does not appear to have been an entirely happy experience. 'I don't like this Saint as much as t'other', she wrote of John Cunningham, adding with characteristic tartness 'and they don't give me enough to eat'.

Later in the century, the Peachey Stone was saved from ever-escalating vandalism by the addition of the still existing heavy ironwork grille.

ABOVE: Writer Fanny Trollope seemingly never forgave Cunningham
for taking over the house she and her family were obliged to vacate
through financial hardship. BELOW: This rare picture of 'Byron's tomb'
(as the Peachey Stone came to be known) shows it as it looked in 1862
when surrounded by long-vanished wooden headboards.

# A CHANGING PARISH

Our natural fascination with the great personalities of Cunningham's day must not blind us to the fact that they represented only a very small part of his parish which, at around 13,600 acres, was the largest in Middlesex.

The activities of Harrow School apart, it was still primarily an agricultural parish, a fact reflected in a low density population of around 2,800, the majority being largely dependent on the vagaries of crop and climate and thus frequently close to poverty.

As Walter Trevelyan, a boy at Harrow, wrote in 1814 in his exceptionally well-maintained diary 'Snowed in morning . . . gave out in church that potatoes were to be sold to the poor for 1s a bushel while the frost lasts'.

Relatively few of the working classes, however, were likely to be in church to hear such news for, as Cunningham was to tell the Select Committee for the Observation of the Sabbath Day, the local farmers did not pay their men until the Sunday morning ('and some of them not even until the hour of church').

The families were, therefore, more likely to go to the shops which, Cunningham reported, 'were very nearly all open for some part of the day', or to the beer houses.

Asked if legally enforced Sunday closure would prompt farmers to pay wages at a reasonable time on the Saturday, the Vicar declared that the farmers of Middlesex were 'of so inferior class' he was convinced they would oppose the idea.

Cunningham was equally scathing about the Hill's Sunday visitors. 'It is impossible for me to say how they employ themselves', he told the Committee, 'except that I may be led to conjecture on the subject by seeing some of them go back drunk in the evening'.

Given the all-too-familiar situation of more people than work (the population was now steadily increasing), the Parish decided to follow the national example of sponsoring carefully selected families for emigration to what was still essentially the New World.

That Cunningham took the closest personal interest in the matter is evident from a shipping brochure sent to him in April 1832 (and now in the Greater London Records Office) on the back of which the shipping company's representative has painstakingly answered the Vicar's many detailed questions about the costs and conditions of the voyage. From this, it seems that the preferred destinations were Montreal and Quebec and the price of conveyance (naturally one-way), £7 10s for each adult and half for children under 14.

In the event, it seems that seven adults and two children left Harrow for Canada though, sadly, nothing further, not even a final destination, seems to be known.

While it would be incongruous to attempt any comparison with the hardships endured by so many of his parishioners, the fact remains that, at this period, Cunningham himself was chronically short of money, not least because he had a prodigiously large number of children, even for an era of large families.

Having lost one son before they arrived at Harrow, Sophia went on to give him a further ten children in the space of just nine years. Sadly — but perhaps not entirely surprisingly — she then died.

Six years later, Cunningham married again, this union producing another three children.

As the Vicarage had now been let to Harrow School, Cunningham also had the expense of maintaining an establishment elsewhere — apparently in a long-since vanished house opposite the old turn-pike in Sudbury Hill near the junction with the present Roxeth Hill.

Cunningham also suffered from some confusion over the ownership of the tithes. Although the customary tithes listed in the endowment of the Vicarage had been paid to the Rector and to the Vicar for centuries, the Harrow Enclosure Act commuted them to corn rents which were by no means easy to collect. (For example, a surviving list of arrears of corn rent at Michaelmas, 1835, totals well over £167).

Matters were further complicated by the fact that there existed an arrangement whereby, on payment of 20 marks a year to the Dean and Chapter of Christ Church, Lord Northwick was owner of the parsonage and glebe lands.

Whatever the rights of the matter, in November 1833 Cunningham was obliged to write what must have been an exceptionally embarrassing letter to Lord Northwick in an attempt to call in the monies he felt were due to the living.

'I appeal as a clergyman with eleven children', he wrote, '. . . to a high and honourable English nobleman without a family'. He claimed he also wrote as one '. . . whose circumstances have latterly driven him from the house he has inhabited for 19 years'. (Cunningham may well have been piling on the agony here for, around this time, he certainly took over the erstwhile Trollope home, albeit as the tenant).

Fortunately, his new and young bride — she was 26 to his 47 — was a daughter of General Sir Harry Calvert of Claydon, Bucks, and undoubtedly had money of her own.

Northwick was never noted for his generosity — Trollope Snr called him 'a cormorant who is eating us all up' — and Cunningham was 'painfully disappointed' at his reply. In a further letter a month later, he reminded his patron that 'the burden of this living has been the great pecuniary calamity of my life'.

This particular correspondence was still continuing a year later by which time Cunningham was insisting that 'in his Lordship's own hand' the income of the living had been given as £820 pa. 'I have never received but £700', he declared, 'and now I do not receive £550'. Then, in a notably unchristian footnote, he adds 'my inability to pay others arises mainly out of the indisposition or incapacity of others to pay me. May they now suffer as I have done'.

It is doubtful whether Northwick ever met Cunningham's claims; however, the Vicar was given the aid of a succession of curates.

One of these, William Bruce, is now remembered simply for being forgetful. It seems that one afternoon c1836 the Reverend Richard Harris Barham (famous as the author of *The Ingoldby Legends*) had just arrived at St Mary's to do some brass rubbings when he came across a disconsolate wedding party without a minister in sight.

So Mr Barham duly married the couple. He then left a little note for the absent-minded cleric. In part, it read: 'It's a very great abuse, Mr. Bruce, Mr. Bruce. And you're quite without excuse. And of very little use as a curate, Mr. Bruce'.

In the early days of his ministry, St Mary's Vestry was virtually the only form of local government that existed and, as chairman of the Vestry's meetings, Cunningham was expected to play his personal part in virtually every aspect of their work.

Obviously this is not the place for a detailed account of Vestry administration — in any event, local historians such as Jennifer Foyle and Kenneth Glyn Charles have already covered the field with considerable authority and their researches can be readily studied at the Harrow Civic Centre Library.

Suffice it to say that, for much of the century, St Mary's Vestry — an open vestry at which every ratepaying parishioner was entitled to vote — was closely concerned with the relief of those in need whether through poverty, vagrancy or bastardy. Crime and punishment (there was a Cage House on the path leading to the Church Fields), fire prevention, the maintenance of roads and bridges, and the running of the Pest (or sick) House on Sudbury Common — all these came within the scope of the Vestry.

In addition, Cunningham seems to have taken a particular and personal interest in education.

Having arrived at Harrow at a time of great local dissatisfaction, following an unsuccessful action against Harrow School in the Courts of Chancery, he promptly set about founding a sound but essentially local alternative to John Lyon's Foundation.

Within a year, Cunningham had opened a parish school — in fact, the forerunner of today's Roxeth Hill School — supported by voluntary subscriptions including, in its first year, his own donation of £20 and some £26 he had managed to extract from Lord Northwick. Even so, the first year's expenses far exceeded the money subscribed and it seems that Cunningham met this — and subsequent shortfalls — from his own pocket.

That there was a need for such a School is amply demonstrated by its rapid growth. A Digest of Parochial Returns for 1816 lists a Day and Sunday School at Harrow with 170 children supported by subscriptions and a Sunday evening school for adults and others, plus a Sunday School at Harrow Weald, all maintained by Cunningham himself.

Throughout his life, Cunningham also addressed himself to the many public health problems arising from a combination of horrendously insanitary surroundings and the kind of primitive medical knowledge implicit in the wording of the 1825 gravestone in his own churchyard. Erected in memory of a Harrow schoolboy, William Lambert, this gives his death as 'typhus fever brought on from sitting in school in damp clothes after playing at football'.

As early as 1816, Cunningham had contributed generously to the deepening of the town well (at the top of West Street) and, when cholera broke out in Hog Lane (now Crown Street) in 1847 and 1848, he was quick to support the demand for a public enquiry. When this, in turn, led to the formation of the first Local Board of Health, Cunningham was the first acting chairman with the School surgeon, Thomas Hewlett, as his deputy.

The first 30 or so years of his ministry were, of course, years of great growth for the parish, much accelerated by the building of Harrow's first railway station (the present Harrow and Wealdstone) in 1837.

As was only to be expected, the coming of the railroad was viewed with decidedly mixed feelings. As early as January 1834 Cunningham urged the London & Birmingham Railway directors to take every means to prevent Sunday travelling. (In the event, there seems to have been a so-called Church Break when the railway services ceased during the hours of church services).

Harrow Vestry, worried about the railway's adverse effect on local agricultural prices, assessed the line at £700 a mile in 1839. Cunningham himself received a total of £275 for the use of some thirty two acres of his land, although his bargaining skills were obviously no match for those of Lord Northwick, who received £3,600 for a mere 11 acres. (In fairness, this presumably included a generous amount for his Manorial rights over the land).

To others, the railroad was a source of innocent entertainment. As Mr Phelps, a master at Harrow School, wrote to a friend, 'It is a great diversion to go down to the railroad station and see the arrival of a train. We saw about 400 persons brought up at the rate of 30 miles an hour.'

Whether as a result of Cunningham's active ministry or the rising population — possibly a combination of the two — the parish church was becoming uncomfortably crowded and Cunningham's attention now turned to the building of daughter churches in the locality.

The first to arise was All Saints at Harrow Weald, consecrated around 1850 near the Chapel of Ease which had been dedicated to St Andrew as early as 1815. Next, Anne and Frances Copland, having inherited Sudbury Lodge and its estate, not only gave the land for a church but met most of the costs of its building (to a design by Gilbert Scott). This new church — St John the Evangelist, Wembley — was designed to serve the-then hamlets of Wembley, Alperton and Preston and part of Sudbury.

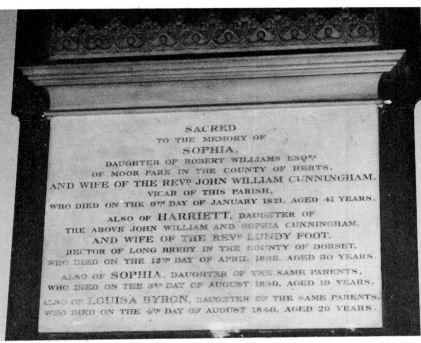

LEFT: High up on the south wall of St Mary's, the Ryves' memorial would undoubtedly have been forgotten had not Lord Byron committed its verses to memory. (Photo: Sophie Powell) RIGHT: A sad reminder in the north chapel plaque of the many personal losses suffered by Vicar Cunningham. (Photo: Sophie Powell)

By this time too, Wesleyans, Baptists, Independents and Presbyterians were all meeting regularly in Harrow though not as yet always on their own premises; however, there was still resistance locally to the provision of a Roman Catholic Church.

As late as June 1855, the *Harrow Gazette* carried a letter signed by 'A Layman of the Church of England' expressing his disquiet. 'Should not such a prospect', he wrote, 'stir up every Protestant to strive . . . to bring his poorer brethren within the influence of his own Church and to see that it is through no neglect of his that any standing room is afforded to the encroachment of an alien faith'.

Those of a Roman faith, however, found a notable champion in Cardinal Manning who had entered Harrow School as a boy shortly after Cunningham became a Governor.

In 1878 — some years, in fact, after Cunningham's death — Manning invited a group of Belgian nuns from the 3rd Order of St Dominic's to Harrow where they took up residence on a site that subsequently became St Dominic's Convent (later, Grammar) School. Some years later, with Manning's continued support, the Hill gained its first Catholic mission in Roxborough Park.

Here a little iron building slowly grew into today's fine church. Given Harrow's history, its name was especially appropriate — The Church of Our Lady and St Thomas of Canterbury.

98

Taken towards the end of his long ministry, this rare photograph of
Vicar Cunningham reveals a man of still imposing presence.

99

Drawn by an obviously amateur hand, this early 1800s view reveals a
plain, roughcast exterior and a totally undecorated roof.

# BEFORE RESTORATION

The full-scale restoration of St Mary's did not take place until around the 35th year of Cunningham's incumbency, a fact that sits oddly with the theory that the church he inherited from Walter Williams was almost literally in a state of collapse.

Nevertheless the Vestry minutes of Cunningham's first years suggest there was much work to be done, but when in the church's long history was this not the situation?

Shortly after his arrival, 'the dangerous state of all the southern part of the Church' prompted the Vestry to call in Mr Cockerell, the Surveyor (presumably the same Cockerell who was shortly to rebuild Old Schools). Two years later, it was 'the dangerous state of a part of the roof' that was causing concern and, in 1815, only prompt action prevented a serious fire after plumbers soldering the roof left work with their stove still alight.

While there is little doubt that we would be able to recognise this early 19th century church as St Mary's, its exterior, in particular, was very different from today.

The detailed illustrations in Lysons *Environs of London* reveal, for example, a building covered throughout in rough-cast, with windows entirely bereft of tracery but glazed in small squares. The tower features both a clock and a sun-dial and the parvise over the south porch is ungabled with a straight parapet and a square-headed window.

There are also plain unbattlemented parapets around the nave and transepts.

This being an age much taken with monumental sculpture, Cunningham's church was already beginning to fill its walls with memorials to the great and the good.

For some years the south transept had been the traditional place in which to remember the departed of Harrow School including, most puzzlingly, a small slab on the floor engraved John Sumner, *born* 7 January 1762 aged four years four months.

Here, too (though much later), St Mary's acquired a memorial to Byron's first Head Master, Joseph Drury, by the well-known Sir Richard Westmacott. Traditionally, Westmacott had no likeness to work from and used as his model an old man spotted in a library in Dover whom Drury's grandson claimed bore an extraordinary resemblance to the late Head Master. The boys depicted are supposed to be Byron himself and his hardly less famous contemporary, Sir Robert Peel.

Popular opinion also gives an intriguing identification to the four figures on the marble tablet by the famous sculptor John Flaxman, which Old Harrovians commissioned in memory of their founder shortly after Cunningham's arrival in Harrow. Idealising the master-pupil relationship, it shows a tutor said to be the Head Master, George Butler, and three boys, supposedly the three schoolboy sons of Spencer Perceval, the late Prime Minister, assassinated while still in office in May 1812.

Cunningham also gave his approval to an elegant memorial to William Osgoode, an English lawyer who became Chief Justice of Upper Canada in 1791 but later returned to the family home at Harrow. His name is remembered in today's Osgoode Hall in Toronto and his tomb still excites considerable interest among Transatlantic visitors.

For a clearer idea of how the interior looked we have to await the appearance in 1816 of Rudolph Ackermann's popular set of prints of Harrow Hill. His *St Mary's Interior* shows that the east window was then glazed in small squares (and partly walled up) and that the chancel roof was devoid of any decoration.

To ease overcrowding at the Parish Church, Cunningham began to build daughter churches, of which the first was the charming All Saints, Harrow Weald.

Other notable features were a long-since-vanished openwork Jacobean screen and an 18th century wooden reredos. The pulpit, too, can be seen in its original form complete with sounding board.

Most interesting of all, the Ackermann print also shows one of the many galleries of the period — that above the north aisle. Erected for the use of Harrow School as early as 1668, this substantial construction actually remained in place until 1888 and, even today, the space it occupied can be deduced from the absence of any plaques at high level on the church's north wall.

In Cunningham's day, this gallery was occupied by the junior boys of the School while the senior boys sat in another large gallery which had been created by blocking off the tower arch and suspending a floor high above the pews.

From a survey made by a Major Heales some time prior to the restoration, we also know that there was, at one time, a further deep gallery at the west end of the chancel which sloped back in successive tiers of seats so that its occupants necessarily faced towards the nave.

As much as any other circumstance, it was the discomfort and impracticality of the School galleries which in the mid-1830s prompted Harrow School to consider a move away from the parish church — a move that, inevitably, was to present Vicar Cunningham with another complex problem.

102

ABOVE: Birds fly around St Mary's spire, seen top right, as one of the earliest trains wends its way to the first Harrow Station. BELOW: An artist's impression of Harrow's first railway line shows the view down the present Headstone Drive from Wealdstone High Street.

ABOVE: Gilbert Scott's work on the second and larger School chapel was much complicated by the School's insistence that he erect it around the earlier building. BELOW: Although his Old Schools extension had been greatly praised, Charles Cockerell's design for the first Harrow School Chapel was almost universally disliked.

# PROBLEMS WITH THE SCHOOL

When John Lyon stipulated that his Harrow Schoolboys should attend service at St Mary's, he could hardly have foreseen a day when there would be more boys than the church could conveniently accommodate or the parishioners willingly tolerate.

By the late 1830s, however, John Cunningham was facing a very real quandary.

On the one hand, as Vicar of Harrow, he naturally felt obliged to uphold John Lyon's wishes. On the other, as a Governor of the School, he was fully cognisant of the School's entirely sensible arguments for seeking the boys' withdrawal from the parish church.

He himself summed up his dilemma very neatly in a letter of May 1839, to the-then Head Master, Dr Christopher Wordsworth.

'My feeling is not personal', he declared, 'but that I am influenced by what I believe is to be best at once for the parish and the school'. 'You would write perhaps the school and parish', he continued. 'I am obliged to reverse the order'.

At the same time, it is hard to escape the conclusion that Cunningham had aggravated the situation by his seeming refusal to adapt his services to the needs of a partially schoolboy congregation. Just about every memoir of schooldays around 1820-1830 — even by those who themselves became noted churchmen — is highly critical of Sundays at St Mary's.

'We had our patience well tried every Sunday by an uninteresting service and a very long sermon of about an hour', wrote the Reverend H. J. Torre, an opinion subsequently echoed by Cardinal Manning who claimed that 'the services in the church were for most of the boys worse than useless'.

If the boys resented their enforced attendance at St Mary's, it would seem a percentage of the parish equally resented the presence of the boys. At a Governors' Meeting in March 1835, the Reverend Cunningham was obliged to report that the parish officers had raised the question of the right of the boys to occupy seats in the church without having paid for them. Cunningham claimed that he had already spoken with the Archbishop, but presumably had received no real direction in the matter for the Governors now decided to take legal opinion.

Two months later, an eminent Counsel of the Ecclesiastical Court found in favour of the School. Nevertheless the seed had undoubtedly been sown for the creation of a chapel for the School's exclusive use accompanied by a partial withdrawal from St Mary's.

Only a year later, Dr Wordsworth informed the Governors that the boys should occasionally form separate and entire congregations of themselves 'when they may be addressed as boys belonging to the same school'.

At this stage, Cunningham seems to have lobbied Lord Aberdeen, the Chairman of the Governors, who recommended a postponement of any move towards a separate school chapel. It was, however, the postponement of the inevitable, especially after the well-regarded Head Master of Rugby, Thomas Arnold, had written to Harrow on the benefits of the chapel his school had recently acquired.

'I would never have the boys go to the parish church', Dr Arnold wrote, 'in fact, we now even bury in the vault under the chapel and confirmations are held always in the chapel for the School alone'.

Before long, Harrow School was finding justification stronger than convenience for the creation of its own chapel; for example, a paper 'for private circulation only' declared that it was desirable that the boys should receive such religious instruction 'as is most appropriate both to their present position as members of a large school and also to their future destination as persons likely to exercise considerable influence over society at large'. These particular instructions, the paper continued, could never be communicated to them as 'a small part of a rural congregation'.

A subsequent appeal for money brought a decidedly mixed response. A Mr G. H. Cavendish promised to forward the appeal to the Duke of Devonshire 'but I will tell you frankly that I almost doubt his doing very much for we have churches to build in Devonshire as you have in Harrow'. The Old Harrovian Prime Minister, Sir Robert Peel, sent money but raised the entirely practical matter of whether the chapel would be put to use, perhaps as a lecture room, on other days of the week.

In the event, enough money (some £3,447 17s 9d) was found for a modest building, the design of which was given to Charles Cockerell who, some years before, had made a splendid job of the reconstruction of Old Schools. Though his design looks attractive enough from old prints, contemporary opinion was far from flattering, one writer describing it as 'a plain hideous red-brick building, something between a conventicle and a racket-court'.

Dr Hawtry of Eton, who was Christopher Wordsworth's brother-in-law, supposedly failed to remove his hat on entering the Chapel, exclaiming he had no notion 'we were already inside the Sacred Edifice'.

In all the circumstances, an element of compromise about both the building and its usage was only to be expected. After its consecration in September 1839 (when Cunningham preached the sermon), it was used by the boys for evensong only. For Holy Communion and Matins, they continued to attend St Mary's.

So, for the time being at least, church and school continued to co-exist with a degree of tolerance and harmony (whatever the views of the boys themselves!).

It was in this spirit that John Cunningham felt able to remind Christopher Wordsworth of the old tradition of the Head Master assisting the Vicar. 'I think the custom has served to cherish a spirit of union', he wrote, 'to remind the master of the necessity of religion as well as learning and the Vicar of the value of learning as much as religion . . . and to unite the School with the parish as all members of one great family'.

On his death, the Parish honoured Cunningham with a chancel plaque,
a memorial window and, most memorably, the much-loved lych gate.

'Ring out the False: Ring in the True.'

# CHURCH BELLS

### EDITED BY J. ERSKINE CLARKE, M.A.

No. 263.—Vol. VI.　　　SATURDAY, January 8, 1876.　　　One Penny.

ST. MARY, HARROW-ON-THE-HILL.

THIS ancient parish church dates from the time of William the Conqueror, having been built by Archbishop Lanfranc, and consecrated by his successor, Anselm. A fine Saxon arch yet remains in the west tower, and some old circular columns between the north aisle and nave. The font, which is Anglo-Norman, has every appearance of being the original one. The greater part of the present building is of the 14th century, and consists of nave, chancel, two aisles, and two transepts, of flint; a chancel-chapel has been added during the present century, and the church restored under the direction of Sir Gilbert Scott. The wooden roof of the nave is beautifully carved with work of the 14th century, and there are many curious and interesting remains of yet earlier work in different parts of the building. Among the valuable

As seen in this 1876 edition of *Church Bells*, Gilbert Scott's restoration
retained the tower clock (although it has long since been removed).

107

Apart from the north aisle gallery and the east window, both subsequently removed, Scott's restored interior has largely survived to the present day.

# SCOTT'S RESTORATION

By one of those neat coincidences which so delight the historian, Gilbert Scott, who was to give Cunningham — and ourselves — the St Mary's we know today, was actually born in the year of Cunningham's arrival in the Parish.

The Harrow commission, therefore, came comparatively early in what was to prove a notable career and almost certainly stemmed as much from his virtues as a churchman as his talents as an architect.

In truth, Scott could hardly have lived in a more ecclestiastical environment had he taken Holy Orders himself. His father was a clergyman; so, too, were his uncle, his mother's uncle and his grandfather, the latter even sharing Cunningham's links with both the Clapham Sect and the Church Missionary Society, being its first secretary.

From Scott's earliest days in practice, church work seems to have been dominant and, by his 35th birthday, he had been concerned with over a dozen new churches including the Church of St John the Evangelist in Wembley.

Unfortunately for our narrative, neither Scott's own writings nor the Vestry Minutes are especially informative about his commission at Harrow.

Of one thing, however, we can be sure. The St Mary's of the time was not in the state of near collapse that has so often been suggested. When the Parish came for the first time under the control of the Archdeaconry of Middlesex in the mid-1840s, John Sinclair, the Archdeacon, was sent to examine the building 'with the view of ascertaining whether it is in a condition worthy of the highly respectable parish to which it belongs'.

In November 1846 he was able to write: 'I had the satisfaction of finding the walls and roof in substantial repair'. Only the floor earned his disapproval, being 'uneven and in some places so dilapidated that the parishioners should be called upon to renew it'.

He was also somewhat concerned about the height of the pews, not so much on aesthetic grounds but for the opportunity they might afford for conduct unbecoming in a church. As he tactfully phrased it: 'The law directs that the Church Wardens should be able to see all that passes in the church and to maintain order in the congregation but this duty cannot be performed when the pews are so lofty'.

It was to improve these areas — the floor and the pews — that quotes were first invited from local craftsmen within a month of the Archdeacon's letter.

Somewhere along the line, however, Cunningham and his advisors obviously decided to use this period of upheaval as the opportunity for a major effort to restore the ancient beauty and dignity of the building. In July 1847, the Vestry was asked to approve an application for a Faculty to spend 'the sum of three thousand pounds in carrying out the repairs and alterations . . . proposed in the plans now laid before the Vestry'.

Though the Vestry Minutes are silent on the subject, the Committee had presumably already appointed Scott as their architect.

At this date, it is impossible to establish just how much of the work was actually done by Scott himself. It was his deputy, John Burlison, who first came to Harrow to survey the church and much of the correspondence that survives is signed 'in the absence of Mr. Scott'. (Scott, however, personally presented his account for the job!)

While it is difficult to establish the precise sequence of work, all of the following improvements seem to have been made.

The unsightly and inconvenient pews were removed and replaced with 'seats of massive oak' and the whole of the floor replaced. The chancel was completely reconstructed with the exception of the arch and the south wall. For this reason, the builders failed to uncover the early lancet windows which, in the event, were not revealed until later in the century.

Henry Young, the lessee of the great tithes, gave a new east window in stained glass and three smaller south windows in the chancel, (all subsequently replaced). The nave roof was also restored.

To compensate for the loss of gallery seating, an aisle, chapel and vestry room were built on the chancel's north side while the chancel's exterior was flinted and new stone buttresses built.

Smaller but hardly less important interior work included the removal of the Jacobean screen, the re-siting (and reduction) of the pulpit and the restoration of the original font whose adventures we recounted earlier.

Finally, 'a good apparatus for warming the entire fabric' was installed.

The Parish, however, was obviously in an expansionist mood and the Vestry Minutes reported that 'the Committee cannot but feel an earnest desire that the work which has been so well begun shall be as well completed'.

Providing they were willing to defer work on the tower ('which might be left as it now stands'), the Committee reckoned that a further £1,000 would complete the outside work and 'render it both substantial and ornamental'. To this end, an application was made to the Exchequer Loan Commissioners for an appropriate loan to be repaid in £100 instalments.

In the event, before the builders finally left St Mary's, the school gallery at the West End beneath the tower had also been removed. (After Scott's restoration, the boys seem to have sat in the west portion of the nave where, according to *The Ecclesiologist* of August 1849, 'the seats for the boys are interspersed with raised ones for the masters'.

The restorers left one gallery in the north aisle although they gave it a lighter, lower balustrade. It finally came down in 1888:

On the outside of the church, the wooden north porch was demolished and rebuilt in stone in order to house the original south door. The latter was then removed — complete with its massive lock and key — from its more exposed original position in the hope (successful, as it proved) of saving it from the ravages of wind and rain.

The parvise was reconstructed with a new gabled roof and window and, finally, battlemented parapets were added all around the nave, providing an infallible way of dating old views of the church's exterior. (In other words, if no battlements can be seen, the print must have been made before the 1847 restoration).

Curiously enough, no record exists of St Mary's being closed during this period of rebuilding although the writer has seen a County Fire Office policy in which J. Woodbridge, builder, and the chuchwardens insure in the sum of £200 'the building of a temporary church and the fitting up therein, timber and tile, a very small portion of thatch, situate at Harrow'.

While one would normally suppose that this referred to the major rebuilding of St Mary's, it is dated January 1849, when the bulk of the restoration would surely have been completed.

As for Gilbert Scott himself, he was to become the busiest architect of a notably busy era, being concerned, it is said, with some 800 buildings, either new creations or restorations. At Harrow, these included both the second (and existing) Harrow School Chapel and the Vaughan Library.

Perhaps inevitably, his somewhat cavalier approach to restoration brought him many critics and, even before Scott's death in 1878, William Morris had proposed an association 'to protect against all restoration work that means more than keeping out wind and weather'. His idea was quickly accepted and, in time, became the Society for the Preservation of Ancient Buildings.

By 1895 *The Builder*, the most prominent trade journal of its day, was somewhat snidely suggesting that it was unlikely that St Mary's restoration had been prompted by anything Scott had actually found in the original building.

Possibly with some justification, the writer claimed that virtually 'a clean sweep' had been made of the interior. 'It is painful to think', he wrote, 'that so much of beauty and genuine devotion was cast out and broken up and to see nothing better come into its place than the tawdry insincerities of the ecclesiastical furnisher'.

Yet we cannot doubt that Vicar Cunningham was well pleased. Nor is there the least ambiguity in the response of those who had worked hardest for this result. As reported in one of the last Vestry Minutes on the subject: 'The Committee cannot but congratulate themselves and the parish at large upon the success which has attended their exertions'.

Soon, St Mary's had not only a new building but was also assigned to a new Diocese — that of London.

For all that this represented a truly massive break with tradition, the decision seems to have excited very little comment or criticism locally. One exception was the 1850 *Handbook for the Use of Visitors to Harrow On The Hill* which claimed that the late Archbishop, Dr Howley, would have been glad to see an exception made of St Mary's 'as it was different from most peculiars; also from old associations'.

At the same time, he 'rejoiced' that he was still connected with the place as visitor to the school.

Cunningham might now have been forgiven for thinking that his major work was done — he was, after all, in his late sixties. Instead he continued his work for another dozen years. But now his problems were smaller. There was, for instance, the little matter of the church clock, described by the local press as the most eccentric of clocks in that 'all hours are alike and none of any importance'.

Many of Cunningham's innovations, such as the annual garden party for the National and Sunday Schools, had become well-loved institutions and, as the *Gazette* wrote, 'the happiness of the children seemed to delight none more than our venerable Vicar'.

Yet if more respect and kindness was daily shown to him in his parish duties, life could still spring some cruel surprises. Having already seen all but three of his many beloved children pre-decease him, in 1856 he received news that two of his grandchildren, 12 year old Rowland and nine year old Gerald, had been drowned while holidaying in Wales.

By his 82nd year, Cunningham was obviously weakening yet he preached at St Mary's until within a few Sundays of his death and, even when he was unable to go out, took Bible classes in his home.

The end came on 30 September 1861. Cunningham was buried in a vault in the chancel but, at the wish of the parishioners, the funeral was a walking procession.

It was, as expected, a moving and impressive occasion as the *Harrow Gazette's* reporter made admirably clear. 'The hearse' he wrote, 'was preceded by six clergymen and followed by the bereaved family, all the masters of the school in academical mourning dress, the monitors of the school, then, by a large number of the inhabitants, professional and gentlemen and tradesmen, three or four abreast, charity school children, volunteers, domestic servants and a hundred poor women, each of whom had been provided with a nice mourning cloak for the occasion'.

In all, there were said to be representatives of nearly 100 organisations for which Vicar Cunningham had worked.

Even today, some of the written tributes still have the power to move us by their depth of feeling and perhaps surprising frankness.

The *Christian Observer* for example, declared that having 'endured gross, malignant, rancorous calumny, he had found rest and happiness and appreciation . . . and silenced by a holy life the false tongue of slander'.

Perhaps most apt of all were the words of the local paper, the *Harrow Gazette*: 'There is not one among us who may not be proud of having been the parishioner and the friend . . . of having received the counsel and enjoyed the society of the late Reverend John William Cunningham REST IN PEACE'.

During Hayward Joyce's ministry, the road up to the Church still had
shops and houses adjoining the School gates.

# HAYWARD JOYCE AND THE PUBLIC SCHOOLS ACT

There could never have been any doubt that John Cunningham would be a difficult man to follow. Yet few could have anticipated the extent of the problems that attended the appointment of a successor.

The parish seemed to have been quite clear in their requirements — they wanted a Gentleman and a Scholar. So a petition was promptly despatched to Lord Northwick, in his role as Patron of the Living, mentioning, with just a hint of self-satisfaction, that the congregation had an 'unusually large proportion of educated members of the upper classes'. For this reason, they felt the new incumbent should be able 'in point of intellectual attainment to rank on an equality with his clerical Brethren who, as Masters of the Public School, number so largely among the residents here'.

It seems, too, that they had a man in mind — the Reverend Thomas Bernard who served as Cunningham's curate in the 1840s and who had given an eloquent memorial address on the occasion of his mentor's death.

The third Lord Northwick seems to have been highly dilatory — obviously a family tradition — in responding both to the petition and the subsequent request to receive a deputation.

More influential voices now intervened. A Mr Hathaway from an address in Lincolns Inn sent his Lordship a letter from one of Cunningham's sons claiming that 'the person whom of all others my dear father would have wished to succeed him . . . was Mr. Bernard'. Even Dr Charles Vaughan, who some seven years before had resigned from the Head Mastership of Harrow, sent a four-page letter of advocacy on Mr Bernard's behalf. Bernard presumably had money of his own for Dr Vaughan wrote of the importance of securing in the Vicar of Harrow 'not only a man of sound doctrine and good example . . . [but] of some private fortune independent of the endowment of the living.'

Whether or not Northwick was aware of the cloud under which Vaughan had departed from Harrow — and the secret was, in fact, maintained well into this century — he elected to ignore his advice.

His Lordship's own choice was one Francis Hayward Joyce MA, only recently ordained and, at that time, Tutor at Christ Church, Oxford.

The appointment, however, was greatly delayed by the fact that Hayward Joyce, although only 32, was seriously unwell. At this juncture, we cannot know the nature of his complaint except that, in October, he wrote to Northwick that 'my illness only interferes with my powers of locomotion'.

There were also problems in the matter of the clerical residence. Cunningham's son, J. W. Cunningham, had recently informed his Lordship (on black bordered paper) that since the lease of Julian Hill had expired the house might now be let. Joyce, however, pronounced it unsuitable. 'From enquiries I have made', he wrote, 'Julian Hill is further from the village than is quite convenient for the clergyman and is bigger than I should require'.

In December 1861, Hayward was able to write that 'the doctor at last announced my disease to be cured'. Yet the very night before agreeing to dine and sleep at Northwick Park, his Lordship's country seat, Joyce was 'compelled by extreme fatigue and sickness' to telegraph his apologies.

In the event, he was not appointed to St Mary's until February of the following year, when he took up residence at Hogarth Cottage in Crown Street.

Fortunately, a ministry so inconveniently begun was to prove a notably happy one. His Crown Street residence brought him into contact with the nearby Barclay family and the town was delighted when he took Miss Barclay as his wife. The Vicar and his bride subsequently moved to the larger Oldfield House in Crown Street until the now vacant Vicarage could be remodelled and enlarged to accommodate a family that ultimately embraced three sons and four daughters.

As a relatively young man, Hayward Joyce can hardly have been content with either the building or the services he had inherited from his 80 year old predecessor but his unusual gifts of tact and patience enabled him to make his changes smoothly and gracefully.

In his early Harrow years, he was naturally much involved in projects the ever-visionary Cunningham had begun. In July 1862, for example, it was his pleasure to welcome the Bishop of Gloucester and Bristol at the consecration of yet another church built for the fast developing area — this time on Roxeth Hill. Doubtless, Cunningham had been influential in the choice of architect, for Christ Church, Roxeth, was again the work of George Gilbert Scott.

Scott's office was also asked to furnish a design for a lych-gate at St Mary's to serve as a permanent memorial to Cunningham's achievements (in addition to the memorial window in the north chapel).

Although the lych-gate is now regarded as one of the treasures of St Mary's, its original welcome was far from unanimous. The *Harrow Gazette* carped about the narrowness of its opening, taking into consideration 'the largeness of the congregation' (a reference, one assumes, to numbers rather than obesity).

A correspondent went even further, describing it as a hideous abortion and likening it to 'a kind of cover to a medieval ink-stand'. 'The sooner some of the present fellows get out at night and pull the thing down', he wrote, 'the better for Harrow'.

Around this time, too, it was discovered among Cunningham's papers that the old Vicar had cherished his own idea of a suitable memorial — namely, a District Church down the hill in Greenhill.

For a while, services had been held in the Greenhill Workmen's Club Room but, in December 1866, a small yet ornate brick church was consecrated in the name of St John the Baptist on the corner of what we now know as Sheepcote Road and Station Road. (The present church was not built until some 35 years later).

It is interesting to note that, while only three churches had previously existed in the parish — St Mary's, the Tokyngton Chapel and St John's, Pinner — nine daughter churches were built within a space of 80 years with the addition of a further 11 in the last half-century.

In 1876, however, much of the energy and resource that had recently been directed into new church building had to be refocussed on St Mary's itself when it became abundantly apparent that work on the tower, left undone at the time of the restoration, could no longer be delayed; indeed, there was every sign that the south-west corner of the church was gradually giving way under the immense strain the tower imposed upon it.

Sensibly, the churchwardens were quick to alert Sir Gilbert Scott who, from the work his office had carried out on the church in the intervening years, was felt to be the man best informed on its true condition. The result was a speedy examination of the tower and a decision that new buttresses and a thorough under-pinning of the whole west side of the church should be completed as a matter of extreme urgency. In the meantime, he recommended that bell-ringing should cease 'lest the vibration should add to the mischief'.

During the early years of his ministry, Hayward Joyce also saw alarming cracks opening in the Parish's ever-fragile relationship with Harrow School.

Unlike some of the controversies of previous centuries, the new debate found Vicar and Parish firmly on the same side. On the other, taking an equally firm stance, were the Governors of the School.

114

The subject, once again, was the rights of parish boys under the terms of John Lyon's will.

Similar rumblings having been heard in towns such as Eton, Rugby and Winchester (wherever, in fact, there were old scholastic foundations), a Royal Commission had been set up in July 1861, to investigate 'The Revenue and Management of Certain Colleges and Schools'.

Harrow naturally figures largely in its deliberations and the Harrow evidence occupied a great many pages of the Report which finally appeared in 1864. The Parish, however, took great exception to its conclusions because, on the vital matter of 'free education', the Commissioners found that 'neither public convenience nor respect for the Founder's intentions . . . demand that it should be kept alive'.

A Defence Committee was promptly formed with Hayward Joyce as its chairman and a petition of some 500 signatures, representative of almost all aspects of Hill society, was duly presented to Viscount Enfield, Member of Parliament for the area, in March 1868.

That same week, Hayward Joyce was also the principal signatory to a circular sent to the authorities of all towns and parishes having grammar schools. The justification seems to have been that, if Harrow were not seen to be fighting, 'it will be hopeless for places of less celebrity to escape the confiscation of local rights which is threatened'.

Certain of the Commission's views were equally abhorrent to the Head Master, Henry Montagu Butler, and his staff, notably the recommendation that no prospective Governor was to be excluded 'by reason of his not being resident or possessing property within the Parish'.

The School was also perturbed at the clause which empowered Governors to make regulations not only on general discipline and management but also on the subjects to be studied.

A further clause — that all Governors must be members of the Established Church — seems to have been largely accepted in Harrow itself but away from School and church it provoked considerable controversy.

The matter was even raised in both Houses of Parliament with, on both occasions, the School putting forward powerful arguments in support. In the Commons, a letter was read from George Butler to the effect that he regarded Harrow as essentially a Church School, sentiments echoed in the Lords by the Archbishop of York, himself a member of the Commission. The clause was therefore still in place when the Royal assent was given to the Public Schools Act in 1868.

To say that the Parish lost the battle is true in the very strictest sense. Yet the Public Schools Act did pave the way for the creation of the Lower School of John Lyon, since the Commission's report had clearly stated that 'some provision should be made out of the revenues of the School for the especial benefit of the class contemplated by the Founder'. (In any event, during his Head Mastership, Dr Vaughan had already opened the English Form where, for a comparatively modest annual sum, parents could have their boys taught not only Latin Grammar but English Composition, Geography and Mathematics).

Throughout the controversy, however, Hayward Joyce and Montague Butler remained the closest of personal friends. When Butler finally announced his retirement in 1885, Joyce wrote that 'from the first day of my coming here [you] have managed to do everything to help me and make my position the happy one it has been. I have never known Harrow without you; and it will be a different place when you are gone'.

Harrow was, indeed, becoming a very different place. Occasionally, however, there were reminders of a far more primitive past — witness the discovery, around 1880, of a curious parchment-like fragment fixed to the old north door. On analysis, it proved to be human skin, evoking memories of a time when it was not unknown for a human hand — legally if cruelly severed from a felon — to be left hanging by the church door as a supposed cure for tumours. (Apparently one used its fingers to stroke the affected part!).

For recollections such as this, the local historian must be forever grateful to the late 19th century passion for information that led to the appearance of that unique publication, the parish magazine.

The first issue of St Mary's magazine was published in April 1893 at a time when the Reverend Joyce was assisted by a kinsman, the Reverend G. H. Joyce, and the churchwardens were J. T. Horley and W. J. Overhead, the latter being the proprietor of the *Harrow Gazette*. The cover proudly announced that all seats were free at every service.

Right from the start, the magazine painted a vivid picture of a highly active, class-conscious Victorian community and, in its busy pages, advertisements for local traders rubbed shoulders with reports of a surprising variety of church-based activities. Many were obviously aimed at easing the burden of the less fortunate in the Parish, including the Provident Dispensary Fund 'to provide medical and surgical aid to subscribers in case of sickness and lying-in'.

In the early issues, it was still possible to read of poor widows supported by church alms making women's undergarments to be sold 'at the cost of the calico'. Typical, too, was the pre-Christmas reminder to 'the children of the better classes' that there were many others 'to whom their old clothes or toys would be the greatest of earthly treasures'.

Moments of humour, however, seemed to be largely a matter of accident such as the notice marrying George Smith to Ellen and Eliza Nobes which, in the very next issue, prompted the hope that 'the Vicar and the lady and gentleman concerned will forgive any scandal we may have unwittingly caused'.

We might also be forgiven for smiling at the curious matter of the disappearing organ — presumably a harmonium, which in 1893 vanished from the Vestry. As the magazine ruefully reported: 'It was supposed for some time to be in the hands of a person in London for repair. But this now appears not to be the case'.

1894 saw two landmark events — the formation nationally of Parish, Rural and Urban District Councils which formally deprived the Vestry of its civil powers, and the celebration of the church's 800th anniversary.

To mark the latter, it was decided to build a new organ chamber on the south side of the chancel at an estimated cost of £843. As it happened, this modest decision was to bring about a far more exciting commemoration for, in preparation for their work, the builders disclosed the remains of the lancet windows dating from the second rebuilding of the church in the 13th century.

So the proposed organ chamber was abandoned and an appeal raised to restore the lancets. Although only three of the original windows were uncovered, a sequence of five windows was ultimately installed, replacing those inserted during the Gilbert Scott restoration.

Of particular interest, then as now, is the fact that the splays of the three uncovered windows all show traces of medieval painting.

Within a few years, another historical discovery was made within the Parish. Workmen altering cottages at the rear of the recently built Mission House in West Street uncovered ancient timber roofing and other features of a medieval building. This was found to be the so-called Pye House, the court of summary justice which had once stood conveniently close to the Church Fields, home to the town's fairs and markets.

As the century drew to its close, the ill health that had dogged Hayward Joyce's early years at Harrow was again causing alarm and, in March 1897, the effects of what was described as a severe chill prompted him to retire. That same year, the parish suffered a further blow in the death of William Winkley. For over 50 years, Winkley had been Vestry Clerk of the Parish, a role which successive members of his family had held for over a century and a quarter.

Although there were memories of 37 happy years to bind him to the Hill, Vicar Hayward Joyce left Harrow for Chester. He never returned, dying in his newly adopted city in 1906.

Greenhill's first parish church, which arose in 1866, was nicknamed the 'candle-snuffer' because of the unusual shape of the tower roof. INSET: Despite the ill-health that threatened to prevent his appointment at Harrow, the Rev Francis Hayward Joyce remained in office for 36 years.

ABOVE: Christ Church, Roxeth, was built in the 1860s to a George Gilbert Scott design, echoing details of his earlier Harrow work on the Vaughan Library. BELOW: Hayward Joyce's choir of 1869 pose in their Sunday best for a formal studio portrait.

118

# THE CENTURY TURNS

In 1897, for the first time in the history of St Mary's, a Vicar was succeeded by a member of his own family — the Reverend Francis Hayward Joyce giving place to his nephew, the Reverend Frank Wayland Joyce.

The younger Joyce, who was always known as Wayland Joyce, came to Harrow after 14 years as Rector of Burford in Shropshire.

Aptly enough, one of his first major tasks was to preside at the dedication of a set of nine clerestory windows given in thankful remembrance of his uncle's life and labours. Beginning with the Council of Clovesho and ending with the School's Tercentenary of 1871, the set illustrates key episodes in the history of the Parish, the church and the school as imagined by the artist T. F. Curtis of Ward & Hughes.

The windows were originally said to be an anonymous gift; however, when the ninth and final window was ready for installation, the donor was revealed to be Edward Scott, Keeper of the Monuments at the British Museum, who had done much valuable work in uncovering Harrow's past.

For visitors with time to spare, the windows offer both a history of St Mary's and something of a miniature portrait gallery. The window commemorating the Grammar School's Charter shows Queen Elizabeth, a bearded John Lyon and a figure presumed to be Sir Gilbert Gerard, while that marking the School's Tercentenary contains portraits of the Head Master Dr Montagu Butler, the Prince and Princess of Wales and one Charles Haddock, the otherwise forgotten Head of School.

A further portrait of John Lyon is now seen in the Victorian stained glass of the south tower window while the equivalent window to the north boasts an imaginative depiction of Archbishop Lanfranc, shown holding a model of the church bearing the old name for Harrow, Herges.

Before the century was out, it had been decided that the whole Parish should be given the opportunity of honouring the late Vicar's memory and subscriptions, from one penny to one pound, were welcomed towards the cost of installing carved boards at the back of the choir stalls listing all his known predecessors.

Next, it was agreed that the churchwardens be similarly honoured. The opportunity came with the retirement of Mr J. T. Horley after an unparalleled 26 years as Vicar's Warden and, in 1903, St Mary's gained an equally valuable set of commemorative boards.

The whole Edwardian era proved unusually rich in projects to beautify the church, including in 1908 the replacement of the east window installed during the Scott restoration with the present window by the highly regarded Ninian Comper. Though some have professed to find its colours unduly pallid, there was wide appreciation of its design which surrounds Our Lord and St Mary with representations of important figures in the history of both St Mary's and the Western Christian Church. Thus St Anselm, holding the primatial cross and a cruse of oil, and St Thomas of Canterbury, bearing the sword of martyrdom, are found in the company of Moses, David, St Peter, St John, St Anne and St Katharine of Alexandria.

Five years later, in 1913, St Mary's gained a long delayed memorial to the late town doctor, Thomas Hewlett, in the form of a renewed and enriched reredos designed by Sir Aston Webb and a new marble floor to the sanctuary. The considerable digging provided ample opportunity to test the age-old theory of an underground passage running from St Mary's to The Grove, the former Rectory Manor House.

To general amazement, some kind of entranceway was, indeed, unearthed although, in all probability, it led only to one of the sealed vaults beneath the chancel. The Vicar and Churchwardens nevertheless declared themselves open to financial assistance for antiquarian research! No-one seems to have taken them up on their offer and, within months, the outbreak of World War I turned all thoughts to sterner matters.

Most of the projects then bringing vast change to the district were halted although the new daughter church of St Peter's, West Harrow (where there had been a temporary building since 1907), was successfully completed. St Mary's Extension Scheme had also envisaged another new church, St Andrew's at Sudbury, but this had to await the return of peace.

Captain E. G. Spencer Churchill, joint lay rector of St Mary's, with Christ Church, Oxford, also had a grandiose scheme for a miniature town of expensive houses. These were to be built on land he had called Northwick Park after his ancestral seat on the Gloucester-Worcester borders but, by the outbreak of war, only Northwick Avenue, Rushout Avenue and Churchill Avenue — all names with a family connection — had been built. Instead, the adjoining fields became a mobilisation site for some 36,000 troops of the British Fourth Division bound for France.

For the first time in history, Harrow itself was not entirely free from threat since German Zeppelin airships were soon flying overhead; indeed, many graphic accounts survive of crowds gathered on Harrow Hill to watch the anti-Zeppelin barrage over London.

Just when these huge war machines were felt to be invincible, a Royal Flying Corps pilot called William Leefe Robinson brought one down with a single machine gun and earned himself both a Victoria Cross and a place in local history, since both his married sister and fiancée lived in Stanmore.

Little, however, survives of the wartime experiences of ordinary church-going folk although C. P. H. Mayo, a Harrow master, has left us a somewhat curious reminiscence in which he describes supplies being brought to the School under the cover of darkness 'lest hungry people in the town should think that we were being too generously treated at their expense': nevertheless, in his view, the boys 'physical strength' had to be sustained since they would soon be required 'to officer the new armies'.

Over 2,900 Old Harrovians did, indeed, serve in World War I of whom 690 were wounded and a staggering 644 (virtually a complete school roll) gave their lives.

One who luckily survived — to become a subsequent Vicar of Harrow — was Geoffrey Woolley, then a lieutenant in the Territorial Army. Only 23 in 1915, he found himself the only surviving officer of his company on the notorious Hill 60, near Ypres, and led his men with such heroism that he too gained a VC, the first to be awarded to a 'Territorial' Officer.

Nor can Wayland Joyce himself have been unaware of the agonies of war for his son was a captive in enemy hands. It was perhaps as a corrective to the prevailing mood of uncertainty that he determined to start a Book of Parish Notes.

By the happiest of coincidences, a gift of money was suddenly received from the Reverend J. A. Cruickshank, a retired Harrow master who, having been married at St Mary's 50 years earlier (by the elder Joyce), sought to celebrate a half century 'full of happiness and blessing'.

A notable local bookbinder, F. G. Webb, was thus enabled to produce two sumptuous volumes in calf-skin embellished with decorative metal corners taken, he claimed, from a 15th century manuscript.

Lovingly maintained by unknown hands for many decades, these books now throw a useful light on a great many aspects of St Mary's recent history, not least the fascinating story of the missing Henry VIII Bible.

As we saw earlier, one of the important consequences of Henry VIII's break with Rome was the decision to place a Bible in English in every church. The St Mary's copy was long thought to be missing but, in his Book of Parish Notes, the Reverend Wayland Joyce tells how between 1900-10, a Mr Daniel Hill, of Greenhill, had several times shown him a Bible of the period 'believed to have been the chained Bible in use in Harrow Church'. As the Notes put it, 'it was discovered wrapped in an old (Dutch?) Communion Cloth of white linen and presumably had come into the possession of the Hill family (Mr D. Hill was the last of the Middlesex Yeomen) when some of them served the office of church warden'.

The Parish Notes make it obvious that some understanding existed that this Bible would eventually be returned to the Church so — and here our narrative must jump a few decades — one can imagine the consternation at the Vicarage when the 18 January 1942 edition of *The Harrovian*, the Harrow School magazine, reported a bequest to the Vaughan Library, of a 'Great Bible printed in 1539 and placed in every parish church'. Significantly enough, the donor was the late Sir Arthur Hill.

Mr M. R. Hewlett, of Oldfield House, wrote to the-then Vicar, Edgar Stogdon, to the effect that Mrs Joyce remembered several occasions on which the restoration of the Bible had been urged — always to be greeted with the answer 'not just yet'. This was confirmed by Mrs Joyce herself who, in February 1942, wrote from Breconshire to recall her late husband saying that 'the sin of sacrilege' was not always understood.

Possibly encouraged by the fact that the Hill family had provided churchwardens for St Mary's from 1784 right through to 1850 (thus giving ample opportunity for the Bible to have found its way into their possession), the Parochial Church Council decided to seek its return from the School.

Then, as indeed now, the real problem lay in establishing that the so-called St Mary's Bible and the bequest copy were truly one and the same volume and the Governors gratefully accepted the offer of their chairman, G. C. Rivington, coincidentally head of a publishing concern, to lift the Bible's end papers in the hope of revealing some indication of its origins.

When these efforts literally drew a blank, the Governors decided that the church's claim was based on insufficient evidence and there the matter seems to have rested.

Today, the School's treasures certainly include a Bible of the period, with a fascinating frontispiece in which the Almighty confides (in Latin) that in Henry VIII 'I have found me a man after my own heart who shall fulfil all my wishes'.

Yet one cannot help but agree with the School's current archivist, Alasdair Hawkyard, that, some 50 years after the controversy, this copy still looks far too clean and new ever to have been in public use in the church.

It is also interesting to note that the Bible in question was recently shown to the public as part of an exhibition of old Bibles in the Old Speech Room Gallery. On this occasion, not one of the visitors seems to have queried its provenance.

Though Wayland Joyce's Book of Parish Notes is silent on the subject, the Armistice of 1918 saw Harrow Hill in the grip of a fierce epidemic of influenza.

C. H. P. Mayo tells us that 'it devastated life at Harrow'. On the Hill, two Harrow schoolboys and a nurse sent to care for them actually died and local medical records reveal a further 30 fatalities in the district though even this sorry toll was not considered 'an unusually large share of the influenza pandemic'.

Sadly, one of the casualties was the air hero, Leefe Robinson, already fatally debilitated by experiences in enemy hands after being shot down in the later stages of the war.

When the time came to dedicate a memorial to the fallen of Harrow in June 1921, it was calculated that the town had lost 1,309 men and one woman — a nurse.

Nineteen months later, a white marble tablet was dedicated at St Mary's to the 91 actual parishioners who had fallen. During the ceremony, the Bishop of Willesden commented with sadness that, on that very same day, the Reverend Wayland Joyce was 'legally resigning his living of Harrow' after some 23 years in office.

Amazingly, as Wayland Joyce himself had commented at his 21st anniversary celebrations, he was only the ninth Vicar of Harrow since the reign of Charles I.

ABOVE: At the turn of the century, Harrow Hill boasted all the shops and businesses typical of a small countrified town. BELOW: The Parish bellringers were photographed around 1905.

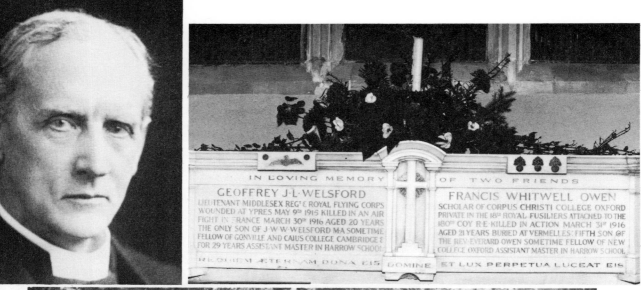

LEFT: Unusually in 1897 a Vicar was succeeded by a kinsman, the Rev Wayland Joyce taking over from his late uncle, the Rev Hayward Joyce. RIGHT: Harrow Hill lost many of its sons during World War I but none more tragically than these two young friends killed in action on consecutive days in 1916. BELOW: This was the scene on a June Sunday in 1921 when the Harrow Town War Memorial was unveiled by Lord George Hamilton, chairman of the Governors of Harrow School.

ABOVE: A top-hatted Rev Edgar Stogdon (Vicar 1923-44) leads the Lord Mayor of London, Sir William Waterlow, to service at St Mary's. BELOW: Perhaps the most notable of Harrow's 'soldier priests', the Rev Geoffrey Woolley (here pictured in the belfry), held both the Victoria and Military Crosses.

# PEACE AND WAR

Given the popular notion that nothing was ever the same again after the 1914-18 War, one might have expected the Hill's first post-war Vicar to be a very different man from his predecessors. In fact, Edgar Stogdon seems to have been more Victorian than many true Victorians. He still maintained a stable at the Vicarage and frequently made his parish visits on horseback. (He always listed 'riding' and 'reading Aeschylus' — though not, one assumes, simultaneously — as his principal recreations).

It is said that he even carried with him a bag of pebbles, from which he would bombard the door of any house he wished to visit, thus saving himself the trouble of dismounting. It is further — and probably unjustly — claimed that only when he was assured that all was well within would he dismount to take refreshment. Were there to be any suggestion of illness, he would call down God's blessing on the house and ride on.

Stogdon's links with Harrow School were also the strongest since Cunningham's day for his father, John Stogdon, had been the School's Classics Master and, from the 1880s, the House Master of West Acre in London Road. Young Edgar, born in 1870, duly received a Harrow School education. At the time, the School roll was notable for the number of boys soon to make their mark in politics and, in 1930, Stogdon was to write to *The Times* that his fellow pupils had included no fewer than ten boys who became Cabinet Ministers, including two future Prime Ministers, Stanley Baldwin and Winston Churchill. This, he proudly claimed, must be a record for any boy at any school.

Ordained in 1895, young Stogdon was very much an exponent of muscular Christianity, being not only a running blue and a University cricketer but also a one-time player for what became Arsenal Football Club. He was therefore warmly welcomed back to Harrow when, after teaching spells at Uppingham and Elstree School, he joined its staff in 1903. He also became Major Commanding the Harrow School Rifle Volunteer Corps where — as *The Harrovian* was later to put it — he helped 'nurture the military ardour of General Alexander and the political leadership of Pandit Nehru'.

It was, however, another aspect of his School career — working with the Harrow Mission in Latimer Road — that helped him find his true vocation and, in 1907, he became Vicar of Holy Trinity, the Mission's Church. Latimer Road in those days was regarded a a 'pocket of poverty and slumdom' and the Harrow boys and staff provided much practical relief for the area including the maintenance of a holiday house in Buckinghamshire.

Stogdon gained further experience of the ministry at Aldenham so, when the Harrow benefice fell vacant in 1923, he was seen as a highly suitable candidate, especially as Captain Edward Spencer Churchill, patron of the living, was known to favour 'military' men.

In the first year, Stogdon had the pleasure of welcoming the-then immensely popular Prince of Wales (later King Edward VIII), to his Church. He was also able to renew acquaintance with Stanley Baldwin when, as Premier, the latter returned to Harrow in 1926 for the dedication of the School's War Memorial.

The weight of traffic and the weight of years having made it unsafe for Vicar Stogdon to continue his travels on horseback, he switched to a bicycle although, ironically, this brought about a serious accident which incapacitated him for several months.

Nothing, however, could quash his lifelong habit of writing to the press, or his sense of humour.

In 1930, when many local voices were calling for the camouflaging of the newly-built South Harrow gasometer, he informed *The Times* that, 'whatever we learned about camouflaging ships in the War, even the President of the Royal Academy could not paint a gasometer to make it look like a tree'.

Stogdon's interest in the local community — he was at one time Chairman of the Harrow Education Committee — remained with him to the very end and, on his retirement in 1944, he moved a few short miles to Northwood. As *The Harrovian* so aptly put it, on his death some six years later, 'Even when he tried to leave, he never got very far'.

Stogdon was succeeded by Geoffrey Woolley, whose previously mentioned Victoria Cross had been followed by award of an MC in 1919 (plus an OBE in 1943). If this were not recommendation enough, he was already known and respected at Harrow School where, following a spell at Rugby, he had been both a teacher and chaplain right up to the outbreak of World War II. His sporting credentials too, were entirely acceptable since he had taken the first Public School Empire Tour to Australia in 1926.

The Patron — still Captain Spencer Churchill — was, indeed, so convinced that Woolley was his man that he made arrangements with the War Office for a virtually immediate release from his post as an Army Chaplain. Woolley arrived in time for the church's 850th anniversary and, more alarmingly, the onset of German flying bombs.

Though it was the fate of some 87% of church buildings in the London Diocese to be damaged by enemy action (of which 10% were completely destroyed), the new Vicar was able to write in his Christmas 1944 message to local servicemen 'the old church on Harrow Hill is happily still undamaged'. Nevertheless he was obliged to add that 'some leaks in the roof tell how it has been frequently shaken'.

Some of the parapets were also in a dangerous condition and, once the war-time ban on bell-ringing was lifted, the bell fittings were found to be seriously defective.

The Vicar also had a few problems with the Vicarage, describing it in his autobiography *Sometime A Soldier*, as 'hardly the place to bring a bride'. (The bride in question was the secretary to the Head Master of Malvern College, whose staff and pupils had been sharing Harrow School's premises for most of the war's duration).

The trouble seems to have been the unsafe condition of at least seven of its ceilings, an unhappy state which was to continue right up to 1948, when part of the Vicarage was divided off into separate flats 'which could be let out and so supplement the reduced income'.

In an age of growing traffic in the air, the thrust of Harrow's spire from Harrow's hill was also creating problems. The 'visibility' that had once delighted Charles II was now seen by the Ministry of Civil Aviation as a danger to passing aircraft and the Consistorial and Episcopal Court of London was persuaded to permit the installation of a system of warning lights.

A yearly rent for the lights of £7.50 was also arranged but, although this sum has been increased over the years, every attempt to impose a truly commercial rent have been met with the response that 'the obstruction light is essentially for public safety and is of mutual benefit'.

Subsequently, the Vicar was alerted that the spire was on fire; certainly, from the School cricket fields, 'smoke' was clearly visible but, on the arrival of the Fire Brigade, the cloud was found to comprise myriads of flying ants.

One April afternoon in 1950 the Vicar was to receive another — and far more agreeable — surprise.

Several versions of the story exist but, according to Woolley's own book, he was speaking on the telephone in the Vicarage when his wife handed him a note reading 'Queen Mary wants to see you'.

At first, he thought it was a joke but Her Majesty, who it seems was in the vicinity with a lady-in-waiting, had decided on the spur of the moment to visit the Parish.

Queen Mary obviously enjoyed her visit for, some six months later, she accepted an official invitation to visit Harrow School for a special performance of the School Songs. This time she

Queen Mary visits St Mary's.

brought with her a song book presented when, with the late King George V, she had first visited Harrow some 38 years before.

Memories of a sadder kind were evoked on Armistice Sunday, 1952, when Geoffrey Woolley officiated at a service marking the unveiling of a World War II memorial at St Mary's. Among its 16 names were those of H. L. C. Woolley, the son of his first marriage, and the two sons of the Reverend C. M. Horley, a former Harrow resident and Vicar of Bisley, Surrey, who shared the service with him.

By the following year, a great deal of the essential post-war repair and restoration had been completed, due in no small measure to the money raised by the recently formed — and still highly active — Friends of St Mary's.

That year, too, on medical advice, Geoffrey Woolley took up a less onerous position as Rector of St George's, West Grinstead.

By then, he and St Mary's shared strong mutal bonds of affection yet he was still not wholly reconciled to the Vicarage. In his farewell sermon, he told the congregation: 'Whoever is Vicar of Harrow now . . . is faced with certain practical difficulties . . . he will have a most lovely house and home to live in but it is quite impossible in these modern times to maintain a house of the size of that Vicarage. Quite bluntly, the size and cost of it was a serious handicap to myself in recovering health when I returned from overseas'.

127

A radiant young Queen Elizabeth smiles at Vicar Blackburne after a brief church tour during her 1957 visit to Harrow School.

# SOMETHING ABOUT A SOLDIER

With the successful ministry of Geoffrey Woolley, St Mary's established a tradition of soldier-priests which was not only maintained by his immediate successor, the Reverend Hugh Blackburne, but also continued uninterrupted through two further appointments over a period of some 35 years.

In the earlier years, at least, it is not difficult to see the guiding hand of the Patron of the Living, Captain E. G. Spencer Churchill, once a Grenadier himself and a much decorated veteran of both the South African War and the 1914-18 conflict. Captain Spencer Churchill was also the last Lay Rector of the Church and, technically at least, the last Lord of the Manor.

How this grandson of the Duke of Marlborough and cousin of Sir Winston Churchill came into this position is, in itself, an interesting story.

In the previous century, of course, the Lord of the Manor had been the Barons Northwick but the 3rd Baron had died without heir in 1887, rendering the title extinct. His widow, Lady Elizabeth Augusta, however, had a daughter by a previous marriage and the bulk of the family estates, including the Harrow lands, passed to this daughter's child, Captain Spencer Churchill.

To a man of the Patron's background, Hugh Blackburne undoubtedly offered a considerable pedigree. A son of the Dean of Bristol, he had served with distinction in the Guards Brigade during the recent conflict and, on the coming of peace, had been made Chaplain of the Royal Military College at Sandhurst.

Blackburne, like virtually every other vicar in St Mary's history, was almost immediately faced with a major maintenance problem, exposed on this occasion when a workman put his foot through part of the north transept roof. In addition to the dry rot and woodworm of previous generations, it now appeared that St Mary's was playing host to the death watch beetle.

No sooner had this problem been successfully addressed than it was found that the movement of the old bell frame, installed nearly 200 years before, was threatening the very structure of the tower.

Once again, congregation and friends rallied round and resources were found to enable a new steel frame, with a capacity for two additional bells, to be installed. A church room was also built at much the same time, prompting Mr Blackburne to forecast (accurately enough) that 1960 would take its place as an important year in St Mary's history.

The next project was to restore the parvise, the little room above the south porch and possibly the site of the old chantry Chapel. Since for years a ladder had been the only means of access, it had long remained undisturbed and, on being cleared, proved to hold much of historical interest. Among items discovered were parish Poor Law Records and a set of weights and measures bearing the names of the churchwardens of 1826.

During Hugh Blackburne's years, it was also decided to lime-wash the interior plasterwork in the hope of recapturing some of the church's early beauty. As the Vicar wrote in the parish magazine; 'The idea of a church appearing in a dim religious light is solely an invention of our grandparents'.

Blackburne was succeeded on his retirement in 1961 by the Reverend Guy Whitcombe who, by an interesting coincidence, had also seen service as Sandhurst's chaplain. The 'newcomer', in fact, knew Harrow well, having been Assistant Missioner at St Michael's, Harrow Weald, in the mid-1930s. He had even played for Harrow Rugby Football Club.

This farewell portrait of the Rev Guy Whitcombe was taken in the churchyard in 1973 when he announced his decision to make way for a younger man after a popular 12-year incumbency.

Two major improvements to the fabric forever mark his ministry at Harrow.

A legacy given specifically to beautify the church — as distinct from repairing it — was used in 1964 to decorate the chancel roof in its present glowing colours. Then, in May 1965, a massive appeal was launched under the emotive but effective name of Spirewatch to repair both the stonework and the spire. So widespread was the publicity it generated that a letter from Battersea and addressed 'The Dean. Harrow Cathedral', was promptly marked by the Post Office with the words 'Try St Mary's Church'.

The Reverend Whitcombe proved to be the last Vicar to be appointed under the patronage of Captain Spencer Churchill as the latter died at the age of 88 in June 1964.

He left no immediate family and his legatees expressed the wish that the advowson, giving the right of presentation to the benefice, should pass to the Parochial Church Council. Its current members, however, felt unable to accept this heavy responsibility and, instead, a triumvirate of distinguished men was persuaded to accept the role.

They were — as, indeed they remain today — the Head Master of Harrow School, the Bishop of London and the Archdeacon of Northolt.

As to the Patron's manorial rights, it is generally believed that they were assumed — if only in a technical sense — by his executors. In 1971, Harrow Council are understood to have suggested that the local authority might legally acquire the Lordship of the Manor but no reply to their enquiry seems to have been recorded.

Tudor-style decoration of the chancel roof belies the fact that the gilded
paintwork is little more than 30 years old, the result of a 1963 legacy.

131

ABOVE: Churchwardens John Lampitt (left) and Dr Michael Edwards
(right) present farewell gifts to the departing Vicar, Freddie White, and
his wife in 1987. BELOW: Wearing her familiar blue cassock, Sacristan
Millicent Harris stands in the aisle of the Church she has helped to
maintain for more years than she may wish to recall.

# THE BLESSINGS OF CONTINUITY

Despite having to face up to problems — arson, theft, vandalism, recession — unknown to most of their predecessors, successive incumbents have yet managed to display that continuity of endeavour which remains one of the great strengths of the Church of England.

The ways in which one generation can build on the achievements of another were especially well demonstrated during the ministry of the Reverend Freddie White who, as a former Assistant Chaplain General, maintained the recent 'military' tradition.

A new side chapel, for example, was created from 'a pewed-up corner' and dedicated in memory of St Anselm.

Two new bells were cast at Whitechapel Bell Foundry for the frame that parishioners of the previous decade had provided. Both new bells were appropriately inscribed, one for the Queen's Silver Jubilee (1977), the other with lines from John Betjeman, the former Poet Laureate who wrote so affectionately of Harrow.

Then, early in the 1980s, the church's long-serving sacristan, Millicent Harris, was inspired to suggest that a replica of the cope of St Mary's great builder, John Byrkhede, should be made to mark both the church's 900th anniversary and the 550th anniversary of Byrkhede's own appointment. The task of recreation fell to a former parishioner, Rosemary Priestman, who spent some six years copying, in the most meticulous detail, every aspect of Byrkhede's cope as clearly shown on his memorial brass.

The result remains both a magnificent garment and a unique link with the past and one can readily imagine the pleasure of the Reverend Freddie White in being able to wear it before he retired early in 1987.

Such high hopes were pinned upon his successor, the present incumbent, the Reverend Ron Swan, that the parish patiently waited a full year while he, in turn, awaited the consecration of a new church in his previous parish of St Barnabas and St Stephen in Ealing.

Given his background (The College of the Resurrection of Muirfield, Yorkshire, and many varied jobs outside the parish priesthood) no less than his wholly undoctrinaire attitude, it was, in many ways, an unconventional appointment.

But then, it must be admitted, St Mary's has become a less than conventional parish. By London standards it is small. There being no house for a curate, it has no paid staff apart from the Vicar; only, at the time of writing, two inestimable lay readers, (currently and coincidentally, both women).

There is also considerable irony in the fact that the famous hill-top situation is no longer wholly an advantage for, in an age of car-owning congregations, it is entirely bereft of car parks. Everyone, without exception, must come to church on foot. Yet, making due allowance for a national decline in church attendance, come they do.

Already, in his few short years at Harrow, the Reverend Swan is providing additional good reasons for coming up the Hill.

Although he rightly tells you that the large and gracious Vicarage 'gobbles up money', a considerable part of the building has now been dedicated as a retreat house where up to twelve people can be accommodated for spiritual refreshment and renewal.

The Reverend Swan has also provided a new chapter in the story of the parvise. Virtually single-handed, he has cleaned, renovated and relit this historic corner in memory of his parents. Then, with gifts from, among others, Mrs Elizabeth Whitcombe, widow of the former Vicar, he has transformed it into an oratory, a place for quiet prayer and reflection.

The Rev Ron Swan, currently Vicar of St Mary's, stands beside the '900'
firework lit on the night of the ninth centenary, 4 January 1994. (Picture:
Sophie Powell)

Though there is little that can be done to change the church's geographical isolation — an
idea for a car park in the Vicarage garden predictably came to nothing — every effort is now
made to associate St Mary's with other churches in the Borough.

Comparatively recent membership of the Central Harrow Group of Churches signifies a
formal link with the area's five churches, including Harrow Baptist Church, the United
Reformed and Methodist Church and the Roman Catholic Church of Our Lady and St
Thomas of Canterbury.

Even as we write, most of Harrow's churches — together with virtually the entire Harrow
community — have plans to make the 900th anniversary a full year not of solemn piety or
insistent money-making but of simple, joyous celebration.

After 900 years, we can safely say that the church that Lanfranc founded and Anselm
consecrated . . . the holy place where Becket preached and Byron, Sheridan, Trollope,
Churchill among unsung thousands have worshipped . . . is very much a living church.

After 900 years, it continues to dominate our landscape, in fact more dramatically than
ever, now that modern floodlighting illuminates its graceful contours for miles around.

Best of all, after 900 years, it is still entirely possible to believe that St Mary's will continue
to grow and develop in order to take as a big a share in our lives as it already holds in our
affections.

Recent floodlighting of St Mary's ensures that the spire remains as
dominant by night as it is by day.

# BIBLIOGRAPHY

Much of the material for this book has been drawn from records relating to the Parish of Harrow and the Northwick Collection of documents, currently lodged at the Greater London Records office; also, the Octo-Centenary Tracts of the Rev W. Done Bushell.

In addition, the following books and articles of local history have proved of value:

*Paintings, Prints and Drawings of Harrow On The Hill* Alan W. Ball
*The Countryside Lies Sleeping* Alan W. Ball
*The Goodliest Place In Middlesex* Eileen M. Bowlt
*English Historical Documents*
*Growth Of The Church In Harrow* Blackburne/Rowles
*The Story Of Harrow* E. D. W. Chaplin
*The Perpetual Curate of Pinner and His Lady* Patricia A. Clarke
*The Parish Registers of Harrow On The Hill* W. D. Cooper
*Harrow Recollections* Sidney Daryl
*Harrow Through The Ages* W. W. Druett
*Pinner Through The Ages* W. W. Druett
*Wembley Through The Ages* M. Elsley
*The Architectural History of Harrow Church* Samuel Gardner
*Early Rectors of Harrow* Joseph Harting
*The Registers of St Mary's* W. O. Hewlett
*Harrow School* E. D. Laborde
*Reminiscences Of A Harrow Master* C. H. P. Mayo
*London and Birmingham Railway Through Harrow* Peter G. Scott
*Harrow School and its Surroundings* Percy M. Thornton
*Harrow In Poetry and Prose* George Townsend Warner
*Harrow School* George Townsend Warner/Edmund Howson
*As I Trace Thy Winding Hill* Elaine Wilson/Dorothy Boux
*Sometime A Soldier* Geoffrey Woolley

The unpublished local history writings of Audrey Boardman, Kenneth Glyn Charles, Jennifer Foyle and Agnes Wyatt have also been consulted with gratitude together with the *Victoria County History*, *Handbook for the Use of Visitors in Harrow On The Hill*, Papers relating to Harrow and Harrow School, the Antiquarian Researches of the London & Middlesex Archaeological Society, the *Survey of Church Livings At The Time Of The Commonwealth*, as well as collected issues of *St Mary's Parish Magazine*, *Harrow Gazette*, *Harrow Observer*, *The Gentleman's Magazine*, *The Builder*, *The Ecclesiologist* and *The Harrovian*.

Other sources consulted, which may be recommended for further reading, include:

*Autobiography* Anthony Trollope
*Anglo-Saxon England* Professor F. M. Stenton
*Babington Plot* Alan Gordon Smith
*Brasses Of Middlesex* H. K. Cameron
*Collins Guide To Parish Churches* Edit: John Betjeman
*The Country Parish* Anthony Russell
*Church & Community* J. H. Bettey
*Doomsday Geography of S.E. England*

*The English Parish Church*  Gerald Randell
*English Society In The Early Middle Ages*  Doris Stenton
*English Society In The Later Middle Ages*  Maurice Keen
*Environs of London*  Rev Daniel Lysons
*Everyman's Book Of The English Church*
*Extraordinary Popular Delusions*  Charles MacKay
*History of Christianity*  Caroline T. Marshall
*History of the Church of England*  Bishop Moorman
*History of the Church of England*  Henry Wakeman
*How Old Is That Church?*
*Illustrated Notes on English Church History*  Rev A. C. Lane
*Indomitable Mrs Trollope*  Eileen Bigland
*Layman's History of the Church of England*  G. R. Balleine
*Lordship Of Canterbury*  F. R. H. DeBoulay
*Life of St Thomas & Historia*
*Novorum In Anglia*  The Good Monk Eadmer
*Life and Death of Thomas Becket*  George Greenaway
*Life, Letters & Journals of Lord Byron*  Thomas More
*Middlesex*  Michael Robbins
*Middlesex*  C. W. Radcliffe
*Oxford Book Of Royal Anecdotes*
*Personal & Professional Recollections*  Gilbert Scott
*The Pre-Conquest Church In England*  Margaret Deanesley
*Reportorium Ecclesiasticon*  Richard Newcourt
*Saints and Scholars*  David Knowles
*Speculum Britanniae*  Norden
*Signposts To The Past*  Margaret Gelling
*Some Antiquities Of Middlesex*  Sir Montagu Sharpe
*Some Notable Archbishops*  Montague Fowler
*St Anselm*  Dean Church
*A Tour Through England and Wales*  Daniel Defoe
*What I Remember*  Thomas Trollope
*The World Of Sir Gilbert Scott*  David Cole

# Index